The Anxiety Reset Workbook

the Anxiety Reset

WORKBOOK

Gregory L. Jantz, PhD

WITH KEITH WALL

The Tyndale nonfiction imprint

Visit Tyndale online at tyndale.com.

Visit Tyndale Momentum online at tyndalemomentum.com.

TYNDALE, Tyndale's quill logo, *Tyndale Momentum*, and the Tyndale Momentum logo are registered trademarks of Tyndale House Ministries. Tyndale Momentum is the nonfiction imprint of Tyndale House Publishers, Carol Stream, Illinois.

The Anxiety Reset Workbook

Designed by Libby Dykstra

Edited by Jonathan Schindler

Published in association with The Bindery Agency, www.TheBinderyAgency.com.

For information about special discounts for bulk purchases, please contact Tyndale House Publishers at csresponse@tyndale.com, or call 1-800-323-9400.

ISBN 978-1-4964-4117-1

Printed in the United States of America

27	26	25	24	23	22	21
7	6	5	4	3	2	1

Contents

A Path of Peace

"I don't sleep at night because I can't turn off my racing brain."

"I constantly worry about the future. Where will I end up? What will the world be like for my kids?"

"When people talk about peace of mind, I can't imagine what that's like—I'm stressed out every day."

"My anxiety is like a bag of bricks I drag around every day. I'm weighed down by so many worries!"

Sound familiar? You've probably said things like this yourself or had similar thoughts slither around in your mind like a venomous snake.

There's certainly a long list of things to feel anxious about: job security, tight finances, health concerns, political unrest, and relationship discord—and feeling anxious in stressful situations is normal and hard to avoid. Most people feel anxious when starting a new job, enduring an audit from the IRS, or giving a speech. Who wouldn't?

But for increasing numbers of people, anxiety is a persistent burden, a debilitating presence that impacts performance and quality of life on a daily basis. In fact, social scientists have labeled our modern era "The Age of Anxiety." With so much brainpower and creativity in our society, I'm sure we'd prefer to be known for living in the age of opportunity . . . or prosperity . . . or innovation. But the fact is, anxiety and anxiety disorders are on the rise.

A recent article in *Medical News Today* began by saying, "For many, anxiety is an ever-present uninvited guest; in our circle of friends, among family members, and in communities at large. It seems to be rampaging through society like a noncontagious cognitive plague, forming a low-level hum that hides in the corners of our collective minds."[1]

No one is immune to the havoc and hardship caused by unrelenting anxiety, and that includes people we consider to be successful, accomplished, and highly regarded. Anxiety does not just affect people struggling with unemployment, financial troubles, serious illness, or legal problems. Anxiety is an equal-opportunity troublemaker, laying siege to people across the economic, professional, religious, and age spectrum.

Living with anxiety, panic disorders, or phobias may cause people to feel that their lives are spiraling downward, robbing them of joy and contentment. It doesn't need to be this way! Throughout my book *The Anxiety Reset*—and in the pages of this companion workbook—my message has been consistent:

- Anxiety may not be *avoidable*, but it is *manageable*.
- Anxiety may be *present* in your life, but it does not have to *dominate* your life.
- Anxiety may *temporarily* cause you distress, but it does not have to *constantly* cause you despair.

Even in our furiously fast-paced and worrisome world, you can live a more peaceful, purposeful, and productive life. You can be free from thoughts, feelings, and habits that drag you down rather than lift you up. You can learn to draw the life-numbing poison out of your past pain, present problems, and future fear.

I am not giving you a pep talk or offering snappy slogans to help you feel better momentarily. The last thing you need is advice that rings hollow or bromides that promise much and deliver little. If you've been struggling with anxiety for any length of time, you have likely heard all kinds of recommendations that didn't bring you much improvement. Worse, you've probably heard plenty of clichés from well-meaning (but unhelpful) people: "Just let it go . . . This too shall pass . . . Hold on to your faith."

As a matter of fact, I know that learning to manage anxiety takes patience, dogged determination, courage to confront painful issues, openness to new ideas, and a commitment to change long-standing patterns of behavior.

Another essential element is needed to overcome chronic anxiety: *hope.*

In my three decades as a mental health professional, I have counseled thousands of people who needed help coping with pain and fear of every kind: anxiety, depression, guilt, anger, addiction, and the emotional scars of physical and psychological abuse. Early in my career, I was often dismayed by the epic scope of battles people waged within themselves and the elusive struggle to achieve true healing. It seemed to me that lasting wellness was a treasure many seek but few ever find.

Then I realized something vital. Many of the hurting people I counseled were eager—or desperate—to overcome their troubles but lacked the key ingredient of hope. By the time these people began therapy with me or sought treatment at the clinic I direct, they had lived with their condition for so long and had tried so many unfruitful treatment options that optimism had all but vanished. Distress and anxiety, usually caused by a variety of factors, were compounded by a fundamental lack of hopefulness and confidence that anything would ever change.

This led me to make hope a cornerstone of all the therapy, speaking, writing, research, and treatment planning I do. In 2014, we changed the name of our Seattle-area treatment facility after clients said, "This is a place of hope." That's exactly what we wanted, and thus the name stuck. We are now called The Center: A Place of Hope. My team and I also adopted Jeremiah 29:11-14 as our clinic's guiding Scripture passage:

> "I know the plans I have for you," declares the Lord, "plans to
> prosper you and not to harm you, plans to give you hope and a
> future. Then you will call on me and come and pray to me, and
> I will listen to you. You will seek me and find me when you seek
> me with all your heart. I will be found by you," declares the Lord,
> "and will bring you back from captivity."

I encourage you to reflect on these life-changing words and embrace them as your touchstone as you pursue your own emotional, spiritual, and physical wellness. After all, persistently anxious people often feel that they are in captivity of sorts—trapped and immobilized by a force bigger than themselves. But God will indeed bring you back. Anxiety-ridden people often do not feel enthusiastic about the future, if they can envision one at all. But God will help you renew your dreams and refresh your energy to achieve them.

As foundational as hope is to true healing, there are many other indispensable steps to take on the journey. And these steps form the twelve weeks of exercises, assessments, and reflections in the pages ahead. In addition to the need for hope, I realized something else many years ago: most anxiety treatments focus on *one* technique to address a complex mental health conundrum. Care providers tend to use their favorite method as a singular fix to a disorder that is never caused by one thing alone. Most frequently, this means taking anti-anxiety medication, seeing a counselor for talk therapy, starting a specialized diet regimen, or participating in cognitive behavioral therapy.

While each of these individual approaches can be helpful and sometimes needed, I believe that lasting healing occurs through a whole-person, multifaceted approach. In my experience, anxiety always arises from multiple factors converging from lots of different directions in a person's life. Treating one thing at a time, with one method at a time, may move you toward healing but will usually fall short of *complete* healing. This is why my whole-person approach includes the following:

- addressing three deadly emotions: worry, stress, and anxiety
- working through the process of forgiveness for hurts and heartaches
- examining the use of technology and making sure it is not contributing to anxiety
- harnessing your thoughts to provide a positive, empowering outlook
- bolstering your physical well-being by attending to proper nutrition, exercise, and sleep
- uncovering hidden addictions
- focusing on soul care and spiritual practices
- minimizing and managing stress
- refreshing your dreams and future plans

These topics are discussed in detail in *The Anxiety Reset*, where I present an array of scientific research studies, psychological principles, spiritual insights, real-life stories, and practical applications. With this companion workbook, I am inviting you to dive in and dig deep into the *reasons* and the *remedies* for your anxiety. Think of me as your guide and coach through the journey. I will point you in the right direction and offer plenty of suggestions, but the challenge is for you to take one step after another through the exercises ahead.

You might choose to use this workbook by yourself, with a friend, or in a small-group setting (I provide suggestions for group use on pages 7–8). You might be someone who prefers to work through the exercises in one sitting, or you might choose to spread the activities throughout the week. You might go back and forth between the book and workbook, or you might complete them at separate times. My encouragement: whatever works best for you, do it! I have created this workbook to be flexible and adaptable for your ideal use and maximum benefit. If you invest yourself in these pages, you will find yourself a giant step toward wholeness and healing after twelve weeks.

No doubt you come to this workbook struggling with anxiety. I tell you with absolute confidence that you don't have to live this way. You can be free to experience peace of mind and to reach your highest potential. You can leave behind the weight on your shoulders that has been pressing down on you and move unencumbered and unconstrained toward a bright future.

Hundreds of my clients who have put the ideas in this workbook into practice are living proof that a whole new way of being is as near as your ability to hope. They have learned, as you can, that life need not be filled with anxiety, depression, regret, and fear. Every moment can be filled with wonder, exhilaration, optimism, and gratitude.

I leave you with these words from the New Testament, fully confident that you will someday soon proclaim them in your own life: "May the God of hope fill you with all joy and peace as you trust in him, so that you may overflow with hope by the power of the Holy Spirit" (Romans 15:13).

Guidance for Groups

Healing can and does happen individually, but *most* healing happens within community. People who suffer from anxiety often feel misunderstood. That's why groups centered on discussing anxiety and sharing personal experiences can be so powerful. Such groups are greatly needed because anxiety is recognized as one of the most widespread mental health issues in the world. Research reveals that

- anxiety disorders are the most common mental illness in the United States;
- forty million American adults—nearly one in five—are afflicted by anxiety disorders; and
- anxiety disorders affect 25.1 percent of children between thirteen and eighteen years old.[2]

Despite the prevalence of anxiety, some people feel there's a stigma attached to this condition, as if they should "just get over it," have more faith, or act happy so they don't bring everyone else down with them. Worse, many people suffering from anxiety feel deeply flawed at their core, falsely believing that their struggles make them different from others or even inferior.

A group centered on the topic of anxiety should, above all, seek to be loving, gracious, and accepting. Everyone on earth struggles with something, whether physical ailments, emotional problems, relationship disappointments, past traumas, spiritual disillusionment, addictive behaviors, and on and on. We are truly fellow travelers on the journey toward wholeness.

With this in mind, here are several suggestions for using this workbook effectively in a group setting:

- It's best for one person to serve as facilitator, setting the tone for the gathering, guiding the discussion, and keeping the meeting focused.
- The facilitator should prepare ahead of time by reviewing the week's exercises and deciding which topics and questions would be appropriate and helpful within a group setting.
- Be sensitive to the discussion process. Try to give everyone an opportunity to speak, and when necessary, gently redirect the focus of those who tend to dominate a discussion.
- Be careful not to put anyone on the spot or make anyone feel pressured to share. The questions and assessments in this workbook cover some very personal and sensitive topics. Encourage group members to share their answers and thoughts if they feel comfortable doing so, and give the freedom to stay quiet if they wish to.
- Use this workbook in conjunction with *The Anxiety Reset* if possible. Ideally, the two go hand in hand, with the book providing thorough explanations of the whole-person approach and the workbook following up with practical exercises. However, each section of the workbook begins with an "At a Glance" summary of the corresponding book chapter(s), followed by an "Essential Ideas" portion, so even those who have not read the book, or who missed particular chapters, can get up to speed quickly and find the discussion helpful.
- The sections of the workbook that best lend themselves to group discussion are "Essential Ideas . . . and Your Insights" and "Dig Deeper." Both of these include several questions and space for group members' responses. Some participants might like to share their journaling response from the "Change Your Story, Change Your Life" section. The bottom line is to use *any* of this material that will be most helpful in engaging your group members in the discussion process.

How Anxiety Affects Your Life

Anxiety may have dominated your life until now—
but you can overcome it!

▪ **Review chapters 1, 2, and 5 in *The Anxiety Reset* book.**

Week 1 at a Glance

Recognizing the far-reaching impact of anxiety in your life—and committing to examine all areas of your life in order to root out factors that are contributing to chronic fear and anxiety—is a great first step toward peace and wellness.

Perhaps, as a society, we would embrace a more whole-person, hope-filled approach to anxiety if we talked more about the prevalence of the struggle and the availability of help. And, in fact, help *is* available.

Through the pages of this workbook, you'll be encouraged to broaden your perspective, embrace healthier thinking, and take proven actions that will help you get from where you are today to where you long to be.

Essential Ideas . . . and Your Insights

1. **There are no quick fixes or magic formulas.** You may already know this. In fact, it's likely you have been struggling with anxiety for a

long time—months, years, or decades—and you've tried different remedies that haven't brought lasting relief.

And yet here you are, because something inside you tells you there is hope and help—and there is. In fact, there is a proven, whole-person approach through which many people have already experienced unprecedented peace and wellness. Are you ready to invest your time and energy in the healing journey ahead?

Your response: What have you done in the past to deal with your anxiety? Why do you think previous attempts failed to yield the results you were looking for? What feels different about this time? Is there a level of investment you are willing to make that you may not have been willing to make before?

_____

_____

_____

_____

2. **There isn't a single cure for anxiety disorders because there isn't a single cause.** A wide range of factors contribute to a person's inability to regulate their fear and maintain natural emotional resilience. These include genetic and biochemical predisposition but also lifestyle conditions such as an unhealthy diet, lack of exercise, chaotic sleep habits, substance use or abuse, excessive time spent online or watching television, and any number of behavioral addictions. Unchecked toxic emotions like anger, guilt, and bitterness also play a huge role in escalating anxiety.

To find healing and wellness, you must be willing to undertake a full-spectrum inventory of your life and be willing to embrace real change.

You must also accept the truth that no one lives an anxiety-free life, nor should we! Fear and anxiety can be healthy—even protective—emotions in the face of dangerous or unpredictable circumstances. But no one needs to live life in the shadow of fear and anxiety.

Your response: Emotions. Diet. Habits. Genetics. Unforgiveness. Addictions. Is there an area of your life you are not willing to examine in your quest for freedom from anxiety? How have you perceived anxiety in the past? Have you attributed it to a single factor in your life? What do you think about the idea that anxiety can have a wide range of factors?

3. **You're not alone, and what ails you is highly treatable.** According to the Anxiety and Depression Association of America, anxiety disorders are the most common mental health issues in the United States, affecting forty million adults age eighteen and older, or 18.1 percent of the population every year. Of these, fewer than four out of ten people seek treatment—despite the fact that anxiety disorders are highly treatable.[3]

    Your response: Have your feelings of fear or anxiety left you feeling isolated and alone? Are you encouraged to know that anxiety disorders are so common—and so treatable? Why or why not?

Taking Stock

How is anxiety impacting your life?

Anxiety is rarely confined to one or two areas of life. Its influence can be far reaching. How often is the quality of your life in the following areas compromised by feelings of fear or anxiety?

1 = very little
2 = often but not regularly
3 = on a daily basis

1. Physical and mental well-being
    1   2   3

2. Social freedom and enjoyment
    1   2   3

3. Romantic relationships
    1   2   3

4. Professional opportunity and success
    1   2   3

5. Parenting
    1   2   3

6. Civic engagement
    1   2   3

7. Spiritual resilience
    1   2   3

Your results:
- If you scored 1 in any category, your anxiety level is likely moderate and tolerable.
- If you scored 2 in any category, your anxiety level is likely manageable but should be addressed through the treatment protocols presented in *The Anxiety Reset* book.
- If you scored 3 in any category, your anxiety level is likely cause for concern and should prompt you to seek guidance from a mental health professional in conjunction with your personal self-discovery and the information provided in *The Anxiety Reset* book.

Change Your Story, Change Your Life

1. What is the story you tell yourself about your history with anxiety?
   Do you think anxiety is an untreatable and unavoidable aspect of
   your life? Or do you have hope that you will find a solution one day?
   Do you believe that change is possible? Write out your story—just
   let it flow without self-editing or filtering.

   _____

   _____

   _____

   _____

   _____

   _____

   _____

   _____

   _____

2. Now write out a different narrative you want to embrace. Where do
   you want to end up? Describe your ideal future and destination.

   _____

   _____

   _____

   _____

   _____

   _____

   _____

   _____

Dig Deeper

1. What do your feelings of anxiety represent to you?

2. When you feel anxious or fearful, what helps you manage those emotions?

3. How committed are you to finding long-term solutions and healthy alternatives to living with chronic anxiety?

4. Are there any benefits you derive from feeling anxious?

5. Do a search of Bible verses that instruct us to "fear not" and write one or two that resonate with you here.

_____

_____

_____

_____

_____

First Steps, Next Steps

Now it's time to get practical. We've explored many issues that prompted you to ponder and process. Let's put those thoughts into action. I'll provide several steps forward, and then it's your turn to determine three additional actions you will take this week.

1. Chapters 1, 2, and 5 of *The Anxiety Reset* identify a total of fifteen actions you can take to begin your journey toward healing in the "Your Personal Reset Plan" sections. If you haven't read the book, I encourage you to do so—and to take the actions in these chapters. Like this one from chapter 5:

> Make a wish list of things you would do, if not for anxiety in your life. Be bold, and be specific. Think back to dreams you had when you were younger—to learn to sail, take an art-history tour through Italy, write a screenplay, or start a business. Considering these things will help you see more clearly what anxiety has cost you—freedom, enjoyment, opportunity, and achievement. The purpose is not to remind you of pain but to fuel your motivation to do what is necessary to reclaim all that you've lost. Give yourself permission to dream big. You are worth it!

> If you haven't taken this action, do it now.
> If you have, what were your feelings after completing the list?

Were you discouraged or inspired? Have you given any more thought to your list—and imagined yourself living the life you long to live? If not, try doing that now.

_____

_____

_____

_____

2. If you have been in denial about anxiety—convincing yourself that "nothing is wrong" while feeling impaired in every area of your life—use the lines below to write the truth. And by the way, write the truth as you would speak it in love to a struggling friend. Here is an example: *The truth is that while anxiety problems are widespread, they are not "normal," they can be treated, and I deserve a life in which feeling fearful and anxious is not a daily occurrence.*

_____

_____

_____

_____

3. Celebrate the step you are taking by cracking open this workbook and embracing the exercises and actions in these pages. As I've mentioned, more than six out of ten people who struggle with anxiety don't pursue treatment of any kind. You're not in that group! You are setting a course and making an investment in your wellness! How would you like to celebrate that?

_____

_____

_____

_____

4. Your turn. What steps do you intend to take this week to move toward wellness?

   a. _____

   _____

   _____

   _____

   b. _____

   _____

   _____

   _____

   c. _____

   _____

   _____

   _____

Closing Reflections

You are not broken because you struggle with anxiety. Fear and anxiety serve a purpose and can provide motivation to solve problems and get yourself out of potentially dangerous situations.

Everyone experiences fear and anxiety in life, and so will you.

By pursuing a whole-person approach to anxiety relief, however, you can experience a greater sense of peace, joy, and freedom in your daily life. You can be set free from debilitating levels of anxiety. You can experience a better quality of life.

Believe that with all your heart as you continue the lessons in this workbook.

Meditate on This Scripture

When anxiety was great within me,
   your consolation brought me joy.

PSALM 94:19

Wise Words to Awaken Your Spirit

Anxiety does not empty tomorrow of its sorrows, but only empties today of its strength.

CHARLES SPURGEON

Journal Your Journey

This week you are going to be trying out new things, taking steps forward, forging new habits, and letting go of old ones. Will these things make a difference? Will you be able to discern any changes in how you feel and what you think?

This space is here for you to journal about the journey. What works? What doesn't? You'll know what to keep doing because you'll have your adventure documented in the pages of this workbook. Use this space to ask questions, make lists, doodle, write about your progress, and record milestones.

Let the adventure begin!

Address the Three Deadly Emotions

How worry, anxiety, and stress combine forces to make you miserable.

■ **Review chapter 3 in *The Anxiety Reset* book.**

Week 2 at a Glance

In war, as the wise saying goes, we must "know the enemy." So we would be wise to get to know the culprits called worry, anxiety, and stress and how they conspire to rob us of power for living.

There are differences between worry, anxiety, and stress, yet they frequently form a "troublesome triad" that can drain the soul and strength from the sufferer. I refer to these forces as a "three-headed monster," which can sound quite threatening and daunting. But the good news is that this monster is menacing but manageable. In fact, you can learn to keep this monster on a tight leash so it doesn't control your life.

While the terms *worry* and *anxiety* are often used interchangeably, there are key differences.

Worry tends to be more specific while anxiety is more generalized. We may worry about a certain upcoming medical procedure (a specific threat), but we feel anxious about visiting doctors (a nebulous concern).

Worry is cognitive, centered in our brain, while anxiety is felt throughout our body. In other words, worry is a mental process while anxiety results in physical symptoms. Since worry is specific and temporary, it is centered in our thoughts. Anxiety, which is more nonspecific and long term, is pervasive—we feel it throughout our bodies (such as headaches, muscle aches, tension in the stomach, intensified heartbeat, and increased blood pressure).

Worry, a learned emotion, is controllable while anxiety can be more challenging and requires different strategies to control. Worry *can* move us to troubleshoot and resolve what's causing us concern. But anxiety is often less controllable. You may experience a general unease about your financial issues or your child's health condition, but it's difficult to convince yourself that all is well.

Stress, meanwhile, is simply a conditioned response to a real or perceived stressor. In that respect, stress is neutral and can go either way. A negative response can lead to pain, panic, or paralysis. But a positive response helps heighten our senses and improve our performance. In extreme, fight-or-flight situations, stress can even save our lives.

The good news about these formidable emotions is that you need not live as their hostage. It is possible to regain the upper hand over what you feel and why. It's understandable if your first reaction is to doubt that claim. Chances are you've been living with worry, anxiety, and stress for so long that they seem woven into your very personality. Don't despair! This is not true. With discipline and concentrated effort—and with support from professionals and others in your life willing to help—you will see dramatic change when you set out to tame your emotions.

Essential Ideas . . . and Your Insights

1. **Worry, anxiety, and stress often work in combination to undermine your peace and tranquility.** It is difficult to say which comes first, but they have a proven and powerful influence on one another. If you are prone to worry, anxiety, and stress (along with other potent feelings), this can compromise the natural resilience you need to keep or regain your balance.

   Your response: How have these three emotions been present in your life over the past decade? In what ways have worry and stress contributed to your anxiety?

_____

_____

_____

_____

2. **Emotions often labeled as negative or bad can, in fact, be positive and good.** We won't come any closer to achieving an anxiety reset if we simply brand worry, stress, and anxiety as undesirable and attempt to ignore them. Like everything else, even emotions typically regarded as negative may also play a positive role in our lives. There are two sides to every coin. In this case, the trick is in seeing the fundamental difference between the side of our emotions that leads to unbridled anxiety, and the side that is healthy and life-giving.

    Your response: Given your upbringing (family modeling, religious instruction, and early experiences), how do you view each of the three emotions we're exploring: worry, anxiety, and stress? How do you deal with each of these emotions?

_____

_____

_____

_____

3. **Your emotions do not have to dictate the direction of your life, including your struggle with anxiety.** It is possible to keep your emotions in balance so that they empower you and do not encumber you. Worry, anxiety, and stress are common emotions that we all experience, and there's no reason to pretend we don't feel them or to stuff them down within ourselves. But how can we know when these normal, natural emotions have turned destructive? The answer lies in the word *empowerment*. If your worry leaves you feeling determined to make some positive change in your life . . . and if stress has opened

your eyes to some area in your life in need of improvement . . . and if anxiety has alerted you to a danger and motivated you to get out of harm's way, then your emotions have empowered you to be stronger, better, and wiser.

Your response: In what ways have worry, anxiety, and stress been positive forces in your life? What changes have they inspired? How can you utilize these strong emotions in your quest to overcome anxiety?

_____

_____

_____

_____

Taking Stock

Assessment to Better Understand Yourself

Awareness is the most effective tool against chronic worry, anxiety, and stress. Use the following questions to see these emotions more clearly—and find ways to manage them.

I feel extremely stressed when . . .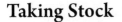

    1.

    2.

    3.

    4.

When I am very worried about something, I feel . . .
    (Include physical sensations and emotions.)

    1.

    2.

    3.

    4.

When my anxiety and stress become excessive, I no longer feel able
to . . .

1.

2.

3.

4.

Four ways that worry, anxiety, and stress can and have empowered me:

1.

2.

3.

4.

Four strategies I know will help to relieve my stress, if I choose to
employ them:

1.

2.

3.

4.

Change Your Story, Change Your Life

1. What is the story you tell yourself about the three deadly emotions—
    worry, anxiety, and stress? How were you raised to handle these
    strong feelings (e.g., suppress them, express them, deny them)?
    Describe some experiences when your emotions caused you trouble
    and times they helped you. Write out your story—just let it flow
    without self-editing or filtering.

_____
_____
_____
_____
_____

2. Now write out a different narrative you want to embrace. Where do you want to end up? Describe your ideal life, free of anxiety.

_____
_____
_____
_____
_____
_____
_____
_____

Dig Deeper

1. Which of the three deadly emotions—worry, anxiety, and stress—has been most prevalent in your life? How so?

_____
_____
_____
_____

2. How has worry been a force in your life? Describe a time when worry was a positive emotion for you (perhaps motivating you to correct a harmful behavior or check in with a friend you hadn't talked to for a

while). Next, describe a time when your worry was counterproductive (such as stealing your joy or your time when what you worried about never materialized).

_____

_____

_____

_____

3. How has stress been a force in your life? Describe a time when stress served as a positive emotion for you (perhaps energizing you to complete a big project or take action on something you had been putting off). Next, describe a time when your stress was counterproductive (perhaps leading you to feel overwhelmed and exhausted without finishing what you needed to get done).

_____

_____

_____

_____

4. How has fear or anxiety been a force in your life? Describe a time when fear served as a positive emotion for you (prompting you to protect yourself in a threatening situation or motivating you to prepare for a challenging one). Next, describe a time when fear was counter-productive (resisting getting close to someone because of painful past experiences, lashing out at someone for a minor mistake).

_____

_____

_____

_____

5. As you consider the causes of your anxiety, to what degree do you think other emotional factors like anger, guilt, and fear (what I call the three toxic emotions) are contributing factors? In what ways do you want to work through these emotions so they don't bring you down?

_____

_____

_____

_____

First Steps, Next Steps

Now it's time to get practical. We've explored many issues that prompted you to ponder and process. Let's put those thoughts into action. I'll provide several steps forward, and then it's your turn to determine three other steps you will take this week.

1. Consider healthy ways to process your emotions—and act on your intentions. This might mean pursuing therapy with a qualified counselor, meeting regularly with a trusted friend, or joining a support group. Describe your plans:

_____

_____

_____

_____

2. Revisit a time when worry, anxiety, or stress created a hardship in your life. Write about the experience, and create a new ending to the story.

_____

_____

_____

_____

3. Write a note to yourself, describing how you would ideally like to handle your emotions.

_____

_____

_____

_____

_____

4. Your turn. What steps do you intend to take this week to move toward wellness?

   a. _____

   _____

   _____

   _____

   b. _____

   _____

   _____

   _____

   c. _____

   _____

   _____

   _____

Closing Reflections

For people struggling with anxiety, the path to healing can seem long and laborious. Therefore, perseverance and stamina are essential. Because worry, anxiety, and stress drain us and make our life seem dark, exhausting, and fraught with problems, it is vital for us to remember that while we are on the path to healing, our minds show us the way, but our spirits energize us and our bodies get us there.

It's true that the pain of this world can produce so much that erodes our sense of joy and optimism. But God is able to take those negatives and turn them into positives. As you consider ways to fill yourself up with life-giving thoughts—an effective way to tame toxic emotions—start with these inspiring words from the apostle Paul:

> Rejoice in the Lord always. I will say it again: Rejoice! Let your gentleness be evident to all. The Lord is near. Do not be anxious about anything, but in every situation, by prayer and petition, with thanksgiving, present your requests to God. And the peace of God, which transcends all understanding, will guard your hearts and your minds in Christ Jesus. Finally, brothers and sisters, whatever is true, whatever is noble, whatever is right, whatever is pure, whatever is lovely, whatever is admirable—if anything is excellent or praiseworthy—think about such things.
>
> PHILIPPIANS 4:4-8

Negative emotions sap us of our mental and physical strength, but the opposite is also true: positive emotions invigorate us, giving us the boost we need to continue through difficult stretches. This week, be intentional about identifying the thoughts that are dragging you down and replacing them with thoughts that lift you up.

Meditate on This Scripture

> Do not fear, for I am with you;
>   do not be dismayed, for I am your God.
> I will strengthen you and help you;
>   I will uphold you with my righteous right hand.
>
> ISAIAH 41:10

Wise Words to Awaken Your Spirit

> Take control of your consistent emotions and begin to consciously and deliberately reshape your daily life experience.
>
> TONY ROBBINS

Journal Your Journey

This week you are going to be trying out new things, taking steps forward, forging new habits, and letting go of old ones. Will these things make a difference? Will you be able to discern any changes in how you feel and what you think?

This space is here for you to journal about the journey. What works? What doesn't? You'll know what to keep doing because you'll have your adventure documented in the pages of this workbook. Use this space to ask questions, make lists, doodle, write about your progress, and record milestones.

Let the adventure begin!

Fortify Your Filters

Screen out negative messages
that amp up your anxiety.

▪ **Review chapters 9 and 14 in *The Anxiety Reset* book.**

Week 3 at a Glance

Without a doubt, there are many hardships we face in life that are due to factors beyond our control. At the same time, we may be tempted to wrongly blame every struggle we experience on things beyond our control.

Understanding the difference between what we cannot control and what we can is important in every area of life. Without making this distinction, we run the risk of living our lives as victims and missing out on amazing improvements, accomplishments, and successes that were within our grasp all along.

This truth applies to every area of life—relationships, finances, health, careers, and our mindsets and attitudes, too.

We can spend our lives complaining about things we can't change, or we can take responsibility for the things we *can* change—and then change them!

I think the idea of taking responsibility has gotten a bad rap because it is sometimes used in the context of owning up to something we did that was wrong and for which we should be disciplined or make amends. This kind of taking responsibility is often painful.

But that's not at all what I'm talking about. I'm talking about taking ownership of our choices—the ones we've made in the past and the ones we will make in the future. In this context, taking responsibility isn't painful; it's empowering.

The truth is, you and I have more power over our futures than we often believe.

This truth applies to every area of our lives, and it applies even to our experiences with anxiety.

Essential Ideas . . . and Your Insights

1. **Many people create or contribute to their anxiety without realizing it.** There are lots of factors that contribute to anxiety, many of which we have no control over. For example, genetics can play a role, as can brain chemistry or childhood abuse. While we can choose how to respond *to* these factors, the factors themselves are not things that we chose for ourselves.

   But many factors contributing to anxiety are, indeed, related to our own choices. We have control, for example, over habits we practice, addictions we embrace, and negative messages to which we expose ourselves.

   Your response: Do you agree that there may be things you are allowing in your life that are contributing to your anxiety? We will be delving deeper into what some of these things might look like, but off the top of your head, what choices may be contributing to anxiety in your life?

   _____

   _____

   _____

   _____

   _____

2. **Habits are helpful—if they're the right kind.** There's nothing wrong with habits. In fact, your brain's ability to put repeated actions on autopilot allows you to focus on learning new things, solving problems, being creative, and making decisions.

   After all, if you had to put the same energy into figuring out how to brush your teeth every morning as you do, say, figuring out an alternative route to work when the highway is closed, you would be exhausted by midmorning.

   So habits are great—unless we never stop to think about them long enough to ask ourselves, *Is this habit still serving me well?*

   The problem is that once patterns form, we rarely give them another thought, and it's hard to see their effects. It's possible that a habit that served us well in the beginning is now creating havoc in our lives. But as long as we continue on autopilot, or remain in denial, we will go on experiencing the havoc without ever analyzing the source.

   Your response: Describe some of your regular habits. When was the last time you evaluated your "autopilot" actions? Do you think it's possible that there are habits you continue to practice that are not improving you but, in fact, could be adding to your stress or anxiety? Which of your habits would benefit from a careful analysis to see if they're still serving you well?

   _____

   _____

   _____

   _____

   _____

3. **Unfiltered negative messages can increase your anxiety.** You may or may not be aware of the amount of negative messaging to which you are exposed every day. And even if you are aware of the messages, you may not realize how much power you have in filtering out those messages.

   Even good news shared on social media can increase our anxiety.

For example, reading carefully curated news about a friend's dream vacation, promotion, or weight loss can leave you convinced that you're missing out on the good life, which can add to anxiety.

Anxiety-producing negative messages don't just come from people around us—we are capable of delivering those messages to ourselves. We do this by engaging frequently in negative, critical, or shaming self-talk.

Your response: Consider a typical day. What anxiety-producing messages do you receive? (Consider your interactions at work, at home, on social media, and so on.) What messages do you tend to repeat over and over to yourself? Are these messages you repeat helpful or hurtful?

_____

_____

_____

_____

_____

Taking Stock

How much anxiety is being created for you by your habits in each of these areas? Use this assessment to determine where you might be able to make some changes. Focus on those areas where you "often feel anxious."

1. Procrastination
   - I rarely feel anxious over this.
   - I sometimes feel anxious over this.
   - I often feel anxious over this.

2. Living in clutter and disorder
   - I rarely feel anxious over this.
   - I sometimes feel anxious over this.
   - I often feel anxious over this.

3. Eating sugary and processed foods
   - I rarely feel anxious over this.
   - I sometimes feel anxious over this.
   - I often feel anxious over this.

4. Spending too much money
   - I rarely feel anxious over this.
   - I sometimes feel anxious over this.
   - I often feel anxious over this.

5. Feeling addicted to your phone
   - I rarely feel anxious over this.
   - I sometimes feel anxious over this.
   - I often feel anxious over this.

6. Being drawn into drama-fueled or toxic relationships
   - I rarely feel anxious over this.
   - I sometimes feel anxious over this.
   - I often feel anxious over this.

7. Feeling unable to set boundaries
   - I rarely feel anxious over this.
   - I sometimes feel anxious over this.
   - I often feel anxious over this.

8. Dwelling on negative messages you give to yourself
   - I rarely feel anxious over this.
   - I sometimes feel anxious over this.
   - I often feel anxious over this.

9. Not protecting yourself from negative messages from others
   - I rarely feel anxious over this.
   - I sometimes feel anxious over this.
   - I often feel anxious over this.

Change Your Story, Change Your Life

1. What is the story you tell yourself about your ability to choose what comes into your life? Do you give yourself permission to set healthy boundaries? Are there toxic people or addictions in your life? Do you acknowledge your ability to change these things, or do you feel trapped? Write out your story—just let it flow without self-editing or filtering.

2. Now write out a different narrative you want to embrace. Where do you want to end up? Describe your ideal future and destination.

Dig Deeper

1. Have you taken steps before to limit your exposure to social media or escape the lure of your phone? Why or why not? If you have, what was that experience like?

   _____

   _____

   _____

   _____

   _____

2. Are there toxic people in your life who regularly communicate negative messages to you? If you can't eliminate these people from your life, how can you set boundaries to stop the harmful messaging?

   _____

   _____

   _____

   _____

   _____

3. What negative messages do you regularly tell yourself?

   _____

   _____

   _____

   _____

   _____

4. What habits are contributing to your anxiety?

_____

_____

_____

_____

5. How intentional are you about filtering out habits, messages, and thoughts that could be making you anxious?

_____

_____

_____

_____

First Steps, Next Steps

Now it's time to get practical. We've explored many issues that prompted you to ponder and process. Let's put those thoughts into action. I'll provide several steps forward, and then it's your turn to determine three additional actions you will take this week.

1. Chapters 9 and 14 of *The Anxiety Reset* identify ten actions to take charge of habits and negative messages that are adding to your anxiety (these are in the "Your Personal Reset Plan" sections of each chapter). If you haven't read the book, I encourage you to do so—and to take the actions in these chapters. Like this one from chapter 14:

> On ten to twelve index cards, write your own list of affirmations. Every morning, thumb through your cards and speak the affirmations aloud. If you can pair your affirmations with a physical activity (walking, lifting weights, even simply standing taller and speaking to yourself in the mirror), they will be even more empowering.

If you haven't taken this action, do it now. If you have, what did you find most helpful about the exercise? What can you do to make these affirmations even more powerful? Can you share them with a counselor or encouraging friend? What new affirmations could you include on your list?

2.   Identify a habit that is contributing to your anxiety. What healthy habit can you replace it with? Identify a small healthy habit to begin to practice in lieu of your own anxiety-producing habit. Practice that habit every day for two weeks.

3.   Do you believe you have the power to change your habits? To build your confidence, identify any bad habit you have successfully stopped—or healthy habit you have successfully implemented—in the past. Write it below. Identify factors that helped you break (or embrace) that habit.

4. Your turn. What steps do you intend to take this week to move toward wellness?

a.

b.

c.

Closing Reflections

Life is about the journey. Never beat yourself up because you haven't "arrived." Every day, enjoy the process of learning how to love yourself, love others, and love God in ways that are deeper and richer than the day before.

Part of this process includes learning how to take responsibility for things you can change, how to embrace better habits, and how to filter negative messages (from others and even from yourself).

You can do this. I believe in you.

Meditate on This Scripture

Do not be anxious about anything, but in every situation, by prayer and petition, with thanksgiving, present your requests to God. And the peace of God, which transcends all understanding, will guard your hearts and your minds in Christ Jesus.

Finally, brothers and sisters, whatever is true, whatever is noble, whatever is right, whatever is pure, whatever is lovely, whatever is admirable—if anything is excellent or praiseworthy—think about such things.

PHILIPPIANS 4:6-8

Wise Words to Awaken Your Spirit

Our Western society is showing its technological muscles in ever more threatening ways, but the experience of fear, anxiety, and even despair has increased in equal proportion. Indeed the paradox is that the powerful giants feel as powerless as a new-born babe.

HENRI NOUWEN

Journal Your Journey

This week you are going to be trying out new things, taking steps forward, forging new habits, and letting go of old ones. Will these things make a difference? Will you be able to discern any changes in how you feel and what you think?

This space is here for you to journal about the journey. What works? What doesn't? You'll know what to keep doing because you'll have your adventure documented in the pages of this workbook. Use this space to ask questions, make lists, doodle, write about your progress, and record milestones.

Let the adventure begin!

Rewire & Reset Your Brain

Calm your mind and calm your anxiety.

▓ **Review chapters 6, 7, and 15 in *The Anxiety Reset* book.**

Week 4 at a Glance

Last week, we examined the power of habits and messages and talked about some ways to improve both.

One of the reasons it's imperative that you take charge of your habits and the messages you allow unfiltered into your mind is that recurring actions and even thoughts hardwire electrical pathways in the brain. That means the more you practice a habit or dwell on a thought, the easier it is for your brain to fall into repeating that habit or thought in the future.

Imagine the deepening rut created by the wheels of a thousand covered wagons taking the same path. It would be nearly impossible for the driver of the thousandth wagon to take a different path, even if he wanted to!

The picture of that deepening rut applies whether the habit or thought is healthy and helpful or limiting and destructive.

So if you are repeating habits and thoughts that contribute to anxious feelings—guess what? You are literally training your brain to foster feelings of anxiety.

The good news is that you can retrain and rewire your brain.

The capability of your brain to grow and change at any age is called neuroplasticity. What this means is that healthier habits and thoughts linked with hope and joy can—with enough practice and repetition—begin to form even more established pathways in the brain than the poor habits and thoughts linked with anxiety. Your brain is an amazing creation, capable of far more than we understand today.

In addition to practicing healthier actions and thoughts, as we talked about last week, it's important to take steps to keep your brain as healthy as possible.

Essential Ideas . . . and Your Insights

1. **It's important to understand the circular relationship between anxiety and the brain.** For example, researchers have found that patients with anxiety have lower activity in brain areas associated with emotional control and higher activity in brain areas associated with processing emotional thoughts. Anxiety hinders the growth of new brain cells, and chronic anxiety can take a toll on brain function.

    To get relief from anxiety, you don't need to understand all the science. But grasping the idea that your brain and your anxiety are linked—and that taking care of your brain is an important step in dealing with anxiety—is imperative.

    Your response: Is the thought that the health of your brain and the level of your anxiety can be linked a new idea for you, or are you already familiar with it? What do you currently do to maintain a healthy brain?

    _____

    _____

    _____

    _____

2. **Your brain can produce too much of a good thing.** When you feel threatened, your brain floods your system with three major stress hormones: *adrenaline*, *norepinephrine*, and *cortisol*. But when these hormones continue to surge indefinitely after the threat is gone, it contributes to a disquieting sense of unrest, increases feelings of stress, interrupts your sleep, and makes you irritable and weary. This is anxiety.

   Your response: Have you ever described your daily feelings as "always waiting for the other shoe to drop"? Do you feel that there is always a threatening event waiting for you around the corner, even when you can't say what that might be? If so, describe what it's like living in that state of apprehension and alertness. Pay attention to the cognitive and physical toll this takes on you.

   _____

   _____

   _____

   _____

3. **Anxiety medication often treats symptoms while ignoring the root causes of the condition.** I'm not encouraging you to stop taking anxiety medication if this is what your doctor has prescribed (and if you are currently on anti-anxiety medication, do not stop taking it until a qualified health care professional tells you it is safe to do so). But I am telling you this so you understand why I take a whole-person approach to health care, including the treatment of anxiety. There are other, and in many cases more effective, methods for treating anxiety, and effective treatment often requires a multifaceted, whole-person approach.

   Your response: Have you tried any whole-health solutions in your pursuit of relief from anxiety? If so, list them below, and comment on anything that has seemed to help.

   _____

   _____

   _____

   _____

Taking Stock

Are you taking care of your brain?

Evaluate the healthy brain habits below, and indicate whether you regularly practice that habit or whether it's something you can improve on. Consider implementing at least one of the habits you marked as something you can work on this week.

I got this   **This is something I can work on**

	Get seven to eight hours of sleep every night	
	Learn new things frequently	
	Reduce stress in my life	
	Exercise for at least thirty minutes every day	
	Wear seat belts and bike helmets to protect my brain from injury	
	Eat naturally colorful foods (orange, red, blue, brown, purple, and green, which have more antioxidants)	
	Drink six to eight glasses of water every day to improve memory, concentration, and more (dehydration literally shrinks the volume of the brain)	
	Enjoy the stimulation and connection of healthy relationships, a sense of community, and engaged social activities	

Change Your Story, Change Your Life

1. What have you believed about the link between your anxiety and brain health? Have you believed the lie that your brain or your levels of anxiety are "set in stone" and cannot be changed? If so, what caused you to think this way? Write out your story—just let it flow without self-editing or filtering.

_____

_____

_____

_____

_____

2. Now write out a different narrative you want to embrace. Where do you want to end up? Describe your ideal future and destination.

_____

_____

_____

_____

_____

_____

Dig Deeper

1. What steps are you willing to take to put you on the path to a healthier brain? What will taking these steps mean for your current lifestyle?

_____

_____

_____

_____

_____

2. Have you taken supplements in the past? If so, which ones, and what differences did you notice after taking them? If not, why not?

_____

_____

_____

_____

_____

3. When was the last time you learned something new? Learning a language, learning to play a musical instrument, and dancing are

wonderful for the brain. In the space below, write a wish list of things you've always wanted to learn.

_____

_____

_____

_____

4. What habits are you currently practicing that are hurting your brain? (Examples could include consuming alcohol, drugs, or sugary processed foods.) Which ones are you willing to give up, and what steps might you take to do so? Which (if any) are you unwilling to give up and why?

_____

_____

_____

_____

5. Are you willing to leave your comfort zone? When you function on autopilot—doing familiar activities without giving them too much thought—your brain isn't challenged. Try doing familiar activities in new ways. For example, brush your teeth in the morning with your nondominant hand. Take a new route to work. Traveling to a different country—or even a different part of your own area—can also stimulate the brain. List some new activities you could try.

_____

_____

_____

_____

First Steps, Next Steps

Now it's time to get practical. We've explored many issues that prompted you to ponder and process. Let's put those thoughts into action. I'll provide several steps forward, and then it's your turn to determine three additional actions you will take this week.

1. Chapters 6, 7, and 15 of *The Anxiety Reset* identify fourteen total actions to take charge of habits and negative messages that are adding to your anxiety (see the "Your Personal Reset Plan" section in each chapter). If you haven't read the book, I encourage you to do so—and to take the actions in these chapters. Like this one from chapter 15:

    > Start taking a high-quality daily multivitamin-mineral-amino-acid supplement now, if you're not already. In addition to a healthy, balanced diet, this supplement will provide your body and mind with the key nutrients on which all the other supplements can build. It's your non-optional foundation.

    If you haven't taken this action, do it now. If you have, working closely with a trusted health-care provider, consider adding another brain-friendly supplement to your daily regimen. Options include vitamins A, C, and E; L-theanine; magnesium; chamomile; lavender; lemon balm; holy basil; bacopa; schisandra; and valerian root.

    In the space below, identify a health care provider who can help you start adding supplements to your diet:

    _____

    _____

    _____

    _____

2. Exercise for thirty minutes today. Studies show that regular aerobic exercise helps alleviate anxiety and depression by changing your brain chemistry, increasing serotonin, and activating the frontal portions of your brain, which are foundational for controlling whether you react rationally (or overreact) to perceived threats. In the space below, write how you might incorporate more exercise into your routine.

3. Here's a fun one. Give your oxytocin a boost by spending time playing with your pet. And if you don't have a dog or cat to pet and cuddle, borrow a friend's! If you were able to do this, write here how it made you feel.

4. Your turn. What steps do you intend to take this week to move toward wellness?

    a.

    b.

c. ....

....

....

Closing Reflections

Even though your brain weighs only about three pounds, it consists of close to 100 billion neurons connected by billions of nerve fibers—and the information your brain transmits along these pathways travels at approximately 260 miles an hour!

Your brain also has the capacity to generate about 20 watts of power, enough to power a low-wattage LED light bulb! And at any given moment, there are about 100,000 chemical reactions happening in your brain.

We know so much more about the brain than we did in past generations, but we still have so much to learn. This much we do know: whatever elevated levels of anxiety you've been experiencing, your brain is playing a role, either by contributing to your anxiety or by performing suboptimally as a result of your anxiety (or both).

Whatever you do to take good care of your brain can make a difference. So renew your commitment today to exercising, eating right, continuing learning, staying social, and taking supplements to support brain health.

Meditate on This Scripture

I praise you because I am fearfully and wonderfully made;
    your works are wonderful,
    I know that full well.

PSALM 139:14

Wise Words to Awaken Your Spirit

I like nonsense; it wakes up the brain cells.

DR. SEUSS

Journal Your Journey

This week you are going to be trying out new things, taking steps forward, forging new habits, and letting go of old ones. Will these things make a difference? Will you be able to discern any changes in how you feel and what you think?

This space is here for you to journal about the journey. What works? What doesn't? You'll know what to keep doing because you'll have your adventure documented in the pages of this workbook. Use this space to ask questions, make lists, doodle, write about your progress, and record milestones.

Let the adventure begin!

Make Peace with Your Past

Healing hurts and heartaches on the path to peace of mind.

▩ **Review chapter 10 in *The Anxiety Reset* book.**

Week 5 at a Glance

Let's start with the basics: *trauma happens*. Some events in life are painful and can leave wounds that go on causing damage to our lives, like ripples disrupting the surface of a pond. Healing is absolutely possible—but it isn't simple or easy.

Why is it necessary to affirm something so seemingly obvious? Because when it comes to healing from crippling anxiety, some common advice you'll hear is not at all helpful. In fact, it is downright wrong. Chances are you've heard some of these gems yourself:

- "It's in the past—just forget it!"
- "Everyone deals with something! Time to move on with your life."
- "When life hands you a lemon, make lemonade!"
- "What do you do when a horse throws you off? You get right back on!"
- "Let go and let God—that's all!"

Don't misunderstand. Most everyone who says things like this is speaking from a genuine desire to help. The problem is that treating anxiety after trauma as if it's trivial—or worse, self-inflicted—only prolongs the process of recovery.

This week we acknowledge that past trauma is real and that it *really* hurts. Then we take a realistic look at what to do about it. Neither anxiety nor the traumatic past that spawned it are a life sentence. Healing is yours for the taking when you are willing to do the work of facing your wounds and treating them appropriately.

Essential Ideas . . . and Your Insights

1. **Step 1: Embrace self-care and safety.** In this first stage, you're making self-care a priority. You are creating equilibrium in your body, emotions, environment, and relationships. You're not necessarily delving into past memories or processing past trauma. Not yet, anyway.

    This is a time to address destructive coping behaviors, get immediate relief from the effects of anxiety or depression, and start regulating emotions such as fear, anger, and guilt.

    Your response: What unhelpful coping mechanisms do you recognize in yourself? In what ways, if any, can you trace them— and other imbalances in your life—to your pain and the need to self-medicate?

    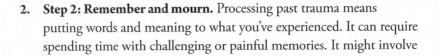

2. **Step 2: Remember and mourn.** Processing past trauma means putting words and meaning to what you've experienced. It can require spending time with challenging or painful memories. It might involve

journaling about the impact of the trauma on your life today. Often the guidance of a counselor or support group is helpful on this part of the journey. In any case, at this stage, you agree to stop covering your pain and to face it realistically instead.

Your response: What frightens you most about taking an honest, eyes-wide-open look at what happened in your past? What do you stand to lose by doing so? What do you stand to gain?

_____

_____

_____

_____

_____

_____

3. **Step 3: Reconnect and integrate.** In this stage, you begin to focus on reconnecting with meaningful relationships and activities. You also begin to integrate the past trauma into your story so that it becomes a *part* of your story, not what defines you as a person. Finally, instead of feeling trapped in an endless loop of painful memories and emotions, you can focus on activities that help you feel empowered and engaged with life.

Your response: What have you given up in your life in order to "manage" your trauma-inspired anxiety? What do you feel when you imagine reclaiming those things?

_____

_____

_____

_____

_____

_____

Taking Stock

As with all wounds, ignoring past trauma is an effective way to prolong the pain and loss. Use the following questions to help bring the past into the light so the healing can begin.

I deserve to feel safe again because:

1.

2.

3.

4.

To flee from my pain, I have allowed the following destructive behaviors to grow:

1.

2.

3.

4.

I deserve to be well and free of anxiety because:

1.

2.

3.

4.

What happened to me in the past left me feeling:

1.

2.

3.

4.

Four things in my present life I can be grateful for:

    1.

    2.

    3.

    4.

Four things I look forward to having or doing again:

    1.

    2.

    3.

    4.

Remembering and mourning my wound now makes me feel:

    1.

    2.

    3.

    4.

What I would do differently if I had to endure my trauma a second time:

    1.

    2.

    3.

    4.

Four healthy ways to deal with my pain:

    1.

    2.

    3.

    4.

Who I want to be now, once my past trauma becomes only *part* of
my story:

1.

2.

3.

4.

Change Your Story, Change Your Life

1. What is the story you tell yourself and others about your traumatic
    experiences? Whom do you blame? A perpetrator? Yourself? God?
    Describe how your life changed as a result of your wound. Write
    out your story—just let it flow without self-editing or filtering.

    _____

    _____

    _____

    _____

    _____

    _____

    _____

2. Now write out a different narrative that describes the healing and
    restoration you want to embrace. Where do you want to end up?
    Describe your ideal life, free of fear and pain.

    _____

    _____

    _____

    _____

    _____

    _____

    _____

Dig Deeper

1. Are you in the habit of framing your identity in terms of your traumatic past? How so?

    _____

    _____

    _____

    _____

2. How do you think your identity would be different if those painful events had never happened? Be very specific.

    _____

    _____

    _____

    _____

3. Are you willing to believe that this alternate identity is still possible? Are you ready to let go of the pain you know for the chance to be that person now? Why or why not?

    _____

    _____

    _____

    _____

4. What does the thought of forgiving others (or yourself) for past wrongs make you feel? What are your reasons for avoiding forgiveness? What reasons can you think of to give it a try?

    _____

    _____

    _____

    _____

5. What good things are present in your life today that have nothing to do with your fear or pain? Name as many as you can think of.

_____

_____

_____

First Steps, Next Steps

Now it's time to get practical. We've explored many issues that prompted you to ponder and process. Let's put those thoughts into action. I'll provide several steps forward, and then it's your turn to determine three other steps you will take this week.

1. Spend twenty minutes writing what you believe about yourself and your future. Then read back over it looking for lies with roots in your past trauma. Pay close attention to harsh judgments and hopelessness. Are these ideas true? Are they helpful? Record your thoughts here.

_____

_____

_____

2. Break the spell of anguish over the past by breaking your routine in the moment. When familiar feelings of anxiety start to appear, disrupt your coping habits by choosing something completely different. Go for a walk, call a friend, write in your journal, bake a cake. How does this change your experience of the fear?

_____

_____

_____

3. Enlist accomplices. Rewiring your thoughts about self-care, safety, reconnection, and integration will be hard—and sometimes frightening—work. It isn't necessary to do it alone. Whom would you choose to stand with you?

4. Your turn. What steps do you intend to take this week to move toward wellness?

   a.

   b.

   c.

Closing Reflections

For many people, moving through these three stages of trauma recovery prepares them to say, "A horrible thing happened. Without dismissing the impact of that hurt or heartache on my life, I can say that I am a stronger person as a result of what happened, I have learned how to create space and care for myself, and I am empowered and free to live a life with meaning and purpose."

Are you ready to make these your words?

Meditate on This Scripture

He heals the brokenhearted
and binds up their wounds.

PSALM 147:3

Wise Words to Awaken Your Spirit

Although the world is full of suffering, it is also full of the overcoming of it.

HELEN KELLER

Journal Your Journey

This week you are going to be trying out new things, taking steps forward, forging new habits, and letting go of old ones. Will these things make a difference? Will you be able to discern any changes in how you feel and what you think?

This space is here for you to journal about the journey. What works? What doesn't? You'll know what to keep doing because you'll have your adventure documented in the pages of this workbook. Use this space to ask questions, make lists, doodle, write about your progress, and record milestones.

Let the adventure begin!

Practice Mind over Mood

Change how you feel by changing how you think.

▤ **Review chapter 11 in *The Anxiety Reset* book.**

Week 6 at a Glance

Mindfulness is getting a lot of buzz these days. It seems like everywhere you turn, mindfulness is being touted as the secret to a content and happy life. But what is mindfulness exactly? Is it simply paying attention? Or is it something more? The answer is both.

If our minds are oceans, then anxiety is a tsunami. Thrashing waves, toppled boats, and debris litter the water. The currents are wild and unpredictable. Who could navigate such a climate?

Anxiety is fueled and fostered by the way we *feel* about our thoughts. We all experience countless thoughts throughout the day. They trickle into our awareness like a steady stream. And for some people, this stream is more like a raging river. As we notice our thoughts, we judge and categorize them:

- *That wasn't a kind thing to think.*
- *I can't believe I thought that.*

- *I know I shouldn't fantasize about that.*
- *If anyone else knew what I thought, they'd be appalled.*

These are all examples of value judgments we make about our thoughts. The combination of swirling thoughts and shame makes for the perfect mental storm. But it doesn't have to be this way. In the pages ahead, we'll uncover practical ways to stop automatically judging our thoughts, viewing them with curiosity instead. Ultimately, this practice will help calm the inner storm and reduce your anxiety.

Essential Ideas . . . and Your Insights

1. **Mindfulness is nothing more than being fully aware of the present moment.** Mindfulness means paying attention moment by moment to our bodily sensations, physical surroundings, emotional state, thoughts and ideas, and spiritual beliefs and contemplations.

   I have learned over many decades of work as a mental health professional that every person is made up of physical, emotional, spiritual, and intellectual components. An individual's wellness depends on these aspects working together in a healthy, harmonious way. Mindfulness helps to integrate those seemingly disparate components.

   Your response: How would you rate your ability to calm your distracted thoughts and pay attention to what's happening right now? When you do, what surprising and often overlooked sensations grab your attention?

   _____

   _____

   _____

   _____

2. **There's a lot more to optimism than simply thinking "happy thoughts."** Optimism is a key ingredient for every content and

successful person. In fact, developing a hopeful, positive, optimistic attitude is far more potent for wellness than many people recognize.

Studies show that optimism has real, tangible health benefits (again, the mind and body influence each other). But can a person who isn't naturally optimistic develop a sense of optimism? Absolutely. Optimism isn't something a person is just born with; optimism can be learned and exercised, like a muscle.

Your response: Think of a time when something happened that caused you to be pessimistic. What might have been different about the situation if you'd chosen optimism instead?

3. **Self-talk is a stream of messages we send ourselves all the time.** We become so familiar with the sound of our own internal voice that we sometimes don't even recognize it as a voice anymore. But the way we talk to ourselves matters tremendously. Our inner voice impacts the atmosphere in our minds, how we view ourselves, and how we perceive the world around us. Anxiety occurs when our inner critic turns up the volume. Some of us were born with a critical inner voice; others experience a slow shift over time or our inner critic comes out during seasons of stress.

The good news is, it's possible to take charge of the narrative for positive change.

Your response: In what ways are you your own worst critic? How does negative self-talk make you feel? What messages would you rather hear?

Taking Stock

It sounds strange to say, but the fastest way to greater awareness is to cultivate a sensitivity to times when you *aren't* aware so you recognize these times sooner.

I often catch myself "zoning out" when:
1.
2.
3.
4.

When something goes wrong, I sometimes accuse myself of:
1.
2.
3.
4.

When I remember to give myself affirmations through positive self-talk, I feel:
(Include physical sensations.)
1.
2.
3.
4.

When I hear someone else talking badly about themselves, I want to tell them:
1.
2.
3.
4.

Here are four things I can do to cultivate a more optimistic outlook:

    1.

    2.

    3.

    4.

When I take a deep breath and become aware, I notice:

    1.

    2.

    3.

    4.

Four clues that could alert me when my mind is not present:

    1.

    2.

    3.

    4.

Benefits I hope to gain from greater mindfulness include:

    1.

    2.

    3.

    4.

When I take a few minutes to simply observe my thoughts, I feel: (Include physical sensations.)

    1.

    2.

    3.

    4.

The idea that I can choose my thoughts instead of being ruled by
them challenges me to:

1.

2.

3.

4.

Change Your Story, Change Your Life

1. Imagine a time when something went wrong and you blamed
    yourself. Write out the story—including all the nasty negative
    self-talk you gave yourself. Just let it flow without self-editing or
    filtering.

_____

_____

_____

_____

_____

_____

_____

2. Now write out an alternate version of that story, one in which you
    chose optimism and self-acceptance instead. What things would you
    say to yourself then?

_____

_____

_____

_____

_____

_____

_____

Dig Deeper

1. Do you believe that the content and quality of your thoughts has a direct impact on your experience of life? Why or why not?

2. Describe some of your life experiences that have led you to take refuge in pessimism as a defense. Is it really true that life is hard? Or is it possible that hard things happen *and* you are equipped to handle them when they do? What can you do to shift your thinking to embrace the latter idea?

3. The material in *The Anxiety Reset* book and workbook has claimed that centering your awareness in the present moment has the ability to calm anxiety. Can you think of reasons why this may be so? Are there examples from your past when you saw this power in action? What keeps you from choosing to focus on the present moment more often?

4. Can you think of times in your life when mindfulness happened spontaneously—when watching a sunset, listening to music, or spending time in the company of a special friend? Describe what that felt like. What steps can you take to choose that feeling more often?

_____

_____

_____

_____

5. To be present means pulling your mind away from its obsession with past regrets and future worries. List the ways in which these things contribute to feelings of anxiety. Now describe why centering your thoughts in the present can help.

_____

_____

_____

_____

First Steps, Next Steps

Now it's time to get practical. We've explored many issues that have prompted you to ponder and process. Let's put those thoughts into action. I'll provide several steps forward, and then it's your turn to determine three other steps you will take this week.

1. Set aside time each day to pay attention to what's going on in the moment. It need not be more than a few minutes. Describe how and when you plan to do this:

_____

_____

_____

_____

2. Start noticing your self-talk. Keep a notebook handy and write down every time during the day that you say something negative to yourself or about yourself. Are these messages true? Are they helpful? Describe your findings here.

_____

_____

_____

_____

_____

3. Anytime you do a chore around the house—the dishes, the laundry, mowing the lawn—try doing it without letting your mind wander. Actively experience every sensation. Then write about how that felt.

_____

_____

_____

_____

_____

4. Your turn. What steps do you intend to take this week to move toward wellness?

   a. _____

   _____

   _____

   b. _____

   _____

   _____

   c. _____

   _____

   _____

Closing Reflections

The mind is one of the greatest assets God gave us to thrive, flourish, and prosper. Our minds can empower us to discover creative innovations, solve difficult problems, and make decisions that lead to a fulfilling life. But sometimes our minds—our thoughts and impressions and perceptions—work against us. When our thoughts are negative, distorted, or out of balance, we become filled with doubt, distrust, and despair. And anxiety.

But this leads to very good news. It is within your power and ability to control and shape your thoughts to be comforting, reassuring, and life-giving. The theme of this entire chapter is distilled down to this: you are not a slave to your anxious, pessimistic thoughts. You are in charge of your thoughts, and you can direct those thoughts to help you rather than hinder you, to propel you forward rather than hold you back.

Meditate on This Scripture

> Do not conform to the pattern of this world, but be transformed by the renewing of your mind. Then you will be able to test and approve what God's will is—his good, pleasing and perfect will.
> ROMANS 12:2

Wise Words to Awaken Your Spirit

> The greatest discovery of my generation is that a human being can alter his life by altering his attitudes of mind.
> WILLIAM JAMES

Journal Your Journey

This week you are going to be trying out new things, taking steps forward, forging new habits, and letting go of old ones. Will these things make a difference? Will you be able to discern any changes in how you feel and what you think?

This space is here for you to journal about the journey. What works? What doesn't? You'll know what to keep doing because you'll have your adventure documented in the pages of this workbook. Use this space to ask questions, make lists, doodle, write about your progress, and record milestones.

Let the adventure begin!

Manage Your Emotions to Alleviate Anxiety

Navigate your thoughts and feelings
to chart a new course forward.

■ **Review chapter 12 in *The Anxiety Reset* book.**

Week 7 at a Glance

Did you know that your thoughts play a huge role in determining your actions and your emotions?

And it makes absolutely no difference if those thoughts are true or false. Don't believe me?

Imagine that you are walking through the woods when you are approached by a growling bear. As the bear rears up on hind legs and waves menacing paws, you register the thought, *I'm about to be eaten*. Fear kicks in. Adrenaline kicks in. You run twice as fast as you've ever run in your life. Heart and legs pumping, you make it out of the woods and to your car. You drop your car keys in the dust. You can practically feel the bear's hot breath on your neck. You fumble with the keys. You open the door. You scramble inside. You gasp for air. Your legs hurt. Your lungs hurt. You've cheated death. You've never been more frightened in your life.

Behind you, in the woods, your best friend unzips his bear suit, steps out of the fur, and stands there laughing.

You were never in real danger (although your *former* best friend might be!). What you believed was never true. But your behavior and your emotions never knew the difference.

Essential Ideas . . . and Your Insights

1. **Fear isn't the only emotion that is driven by what we believe.** Anxiety, depression, joy, hope, confidence, shame—our thoughts and beliefs can fuel all of these emotions and more.

    This is one of the most powerful reasons why breaking free from the grip of anxiety can seem so hard to do. In short, our own mental habits can exacerbate—if not even create—the problem. Most of the time this happens beyond our conscious awareness, like a program running in the background on your computer, out of sight, but very much in charge of your experience.

    All of which is bad news and good news.

    The bad news is that we can go years—even a lifetime—without realizing the link between our thoughts and our actions/emotions.

    The good news is that once we realize what is happening, it is very much within our power to change courses—and change our lives in the process.

    Your response: Have you ever had an experience where you reacted to something that turned out not to be true? What happened, and what was the result?

    _____

    _____

    _____

    _____

    _____

    _____

2. **Managing your emotions to alleviate anxiety often starts with managing your thoughts and beliefs.** Cognitive behavioral therapy (CBT) is a powerful therapy technique that recognizes the link

between our thoughts (cognition), our actions (behavior), and our emotions.

When our thoughts and beliefs are out of whack, the theory goes, then our actions and emotions will be too.

Some forms of psychotherapy focus on a person's past to unravel the root of today's struggles. CBT focuses on current thought patterns that, if altered, can reap nearly immediate improvements in a person's quality of life.

Your response: We can't change the past. What we can change, however, is our perception and interpretation of past events. Are there events in your past that you believe are fueling your anxiety today? What are those events? What do you think about the idea that healing damaging thoughts and beliefs you've been hanging on to from your past can bring you greater peace?

_____

_____

_____

_____

3. **"Dysfunctional assumptions" is the name given by psychologists to negative and inaccurate self-talk.** These are the kinds of thoughts and beliefs that can fuel anxiety (and also fuel choices and actions that seem to reinforce the dysfunctional beliefs). Here are some examples of dysfunctional assumptions:

- Career: *Things never work out for me, so why bother trying anymore?*

- Health: *Odds are good I'll get cancer at some time in my life.*

- Parenting: *The world is full of bad people who want to hurt my kids.*

- Finances: *I'm no good with money. I never will be.*

If much of the fear and anxiety you suffer is the result of misguided— or flat-out false—thoughts and assumptions, no wonder changing how you think can directly change your life!

Your response: Do any of the above examples of "dysfunctional assumptions" sound familiar? Have you ever jumped to similar assumptions? Like what?

_____

_____

_____

_____

Taking Stock

How willing are you to objectively examine your assumptions? On a scale of one to ten, how true are the following statements?

1   2   3   4   5   6   7   8   9   10

COMPLETELY FALSE   COMPLETELY TRUE

1. I believe things about myself, my life, or others that make me feel sad or anxious.

    1   2   3   4   5   6   7   8   9   10

2. If beliefs I hold are false and contributing to my anxiety, I am willing to reevaluate those beliefs.

    1   2   3   4   5   6   7   8   9   10

3. The things I believe influence my actions and emotions.

    1   2   3   4   5   6   7   8   9   10

4. The idea of letting go of some of my beliefs—even if they are untrue—fills me with anxiety.

    1   2   3   4   5   6   7   8   9   10

5. I am willing to change my thoughts if it improves my life.

    1   2   3   4   5   6   7   8   9   10

Change Your Story, Change Your Life

1. Describe the dysfunctional assumptions you have embraced about yourself. How have they contributed to the story you tell about yourself? Write it all out—just let it flow without self-editing or filtering.

_____

_____

_____

_____

_____

_____

2. Now write out a different narrative you want to embrace. Where do you want to end up? Describe your ideal future and destination.

_____

_____

_____

_____

_____

Dig Deeper

1. Can you remember a time when you did not struggle with anxiety? If so, when was that? What did that feel like?

_____

_____

_____

_____

2. What did you believe about yourself during that season? What did your life look like?

_____

_____

_____

_____

_____

3. When did your struggle with anxiety begin? Can you identify a shift in your thoughts or beliefs around that time? What happened?

_____

_____

_____

_____

_____

4. Write down three to seven recurring thoughts you have that contribute to feelings of anxiety.

_____

_____

_____

_____

_____

5. What might your life look like if you knew these things were not true?

_____

_____

_____

_____

_____

First Steps, Next Steps

Now it's time to get practical. We've explored many issues that prompted you to ponder and process. Let's put those thoughts into action. I'll provide several steps forward, and then it's your turn to determine three additional actions you will take this week.

1. Chapter 12 of *The Anxiety Reset* identifies five actions for you to take charge of the misguided thoughts fueling your behaviors and emotions. If you haven't read the book, I encourage you to do so—and to take the actions in this chapter. Like this one:

    > So far, by noticing your thoughts, recording them, and rewriting them, you've still remained in the privacy of your own mind. However, there is real power in speaking these things out loud as well. It's important to choose someone who will listen but not judge; who will support you without the need to add their voice in intervention. Sometimes just hearing yourself say the distorted beliefs that have been your mental default for years is enough to help you see through them—and to know what you'd like to believe instead.

    If you haven't taken this action, do it now.

    If you have, what was that like? Was the person you spoke with able to help you see the distortion in the things you have believed? Even if the person with whom you shared was not able to shed the light of truth on the lies you've believed, what was it like hearing yourself speak them aloud? Did a part of you rebel against the untruths you spoke aloud? Did speaking your deepest fears begin to decrease their power over you?

2. How do you typically respond when you feel anxious? What actions do you take? Close your eyes and envision yourself experiencing anxiety, then taking a completely different action. Envision yourself breathing deeply, inhaling peace and exhaling anxiety. Imagine you are watching a video, and in this video you respond in a healthier way to your feeling of anxiety. Your anxiety begins to diminish until it is completely gone. Jot down a few thoughts and feelings following that exercise.

    _____

    _____

    _____

    _____

    _____

3. We all have people in our lives who believe lies about themselves, their lives, or other people. We can see the truth—why can't they? What advice would you give to someone you loved who had limiting, dysfunctional beliefs about themselves? And how can you apply that advice to yourself?

    _____

    _____

    _____

    _____

    _____

4. Your turn. What steps do you intend to take this week to move toward wellness?

    a. _____

    _____

    _____

    _____

b. ....

....

....

....

c. ....

....

....

....

Closing Reflections

When dysfunctional assumptions fuel our actions and our emotions, we can find ourselves behaving in ways—and feeling things—that appear to support our beliefs. In this way, our dysfunctional assumptions become self-fulfilling.

Again, this doesn't mean they are true.

Going back to our bear illustration at the start of this week, if you believed you were about to be attacked by a real bear and you ran through the woods in sheer panic, it would be easy to think back on the experience of panicked running—and your overwhelming feelings of fear—as proof that your belief was true.

Stopping the circular pattern of beliefs, actions, emotions, beliefs (and so on) is a critical step in gaining freedom from debilitating anxiety.

Meditate on This Scripture

"I know the plans I have for you," declares the LORD, "plans to prosper you and not to harm you, plans to give you hope and a future."
JEREMIAH 29:11

Wise Words to Awaken Your Spirit

Let go of the thoughts that don't make you strong.
KAREN SALMANSOHN

Journal Your Journey

This week you are going to be trying out new things, taking steps forward, forging new habits, and letting go of old ones. Will these things make a difference? Will you be able to discern any changes in how you feel and what you think?

This space is here for you to journal about the journey. What works? What doesn't? You'll know what to keep doing because you'll have your adventure documented in the pages of this workbook. Use this space to ask questions, make lists, doodle, write about your progress, and record milestones.

Let the adventure begin!

Bolster Your Body

Here's how to reset your physical strength and wellness.

▪ **Review chapter 13 in *The Anxiety Reset* book.**

Week 8 at a Glance

Research showing the link between your physical and emotional health continues to grow.

For example, we are just now beginning to understand the connection between the brain and the intestinal tract. In fact, this connection is so strong that the gut has been labeled "the second brain." This is because the health of your gut microbiome—the ecosystem of friendly and unfriendly bacteria that live in your intestines—impacts your mood, motivation, and even cognitive function.

This week, we're going to look at the circular relationship between physical health and anxiety and how poor health fuels anxiety and vice versa.

We're also going to look at some practical ways you can improve your health, including your gut health.

Essential Ideas . . . and Your Insights

1. **Anxiety puts stress on your body.** As you've wrestled with anxieties large and small, you may have already recognized the impact on your body. Perhaps your heart races and your blood pressure rises. Your anxiety may result in headaches, muscle tension, exhaustion, or nausea. It can keep you from a good night's sleep. You may even have experienced a surge in adrenaline as your body goes into fight-or-flight mode.

    Chronic anxiety is hard on your health. But it's a two-way street, because poor health can exacerbate your anxiety.

    Stopping the cycle is important. So where can you start?

    Chances are, you've been trying to control your emotions—and in particular feelings of anxiety—for years. And managing your emotions isn't a bad thing.

    In this chapter, however, we're going to suggest taking a break from that familiar battle and focusing on your health for a while. You may find it a welcome change as you stop focusing on your emotions and instead tackle a seemingly simpler problem, like going to bed earlier or drinking more water.

    I'm not saying that embracing healthier habits is simple. Change of any kind requires intentionality and practice. What I am saying is that the benefit will be well worth the effort.

    Your response: Does focusing on taking better care of your health feel like a welcome change of pace, or does it add to your feelings of anxiety and overwhelm? Why do you think you answered the way you did?

    _____

    _____

    _____

    _____

    _____

    _____

2. **There are a number of things you can do to bolster your body—which will in turn improve your mood and emotions.** Ways to take care of your health that will improve your overall mood include fueling, hydrating, moving, and resting your body; replenishing your body with nutrients and supplements; and balancing your body's gut health.

   Your response: When you are feeling anxious, how likely are you to look at deficits in how you are taking care of your body as a possible contributor to your feelings? What do you think would happen if you made a habit of asking yourself, *Wait . . . is my world* really *falling apart? Or is it possible that things feel worse than they really are because I am tired or hungry or dehydrated?*

   _____

   _____

   _____

   _____

3. **Just as the health of your body impacts your emotions, your emotions impact the health of your body.** Living with anxiety is like living on high idle. Your body can't help but be impaired by a frequent anxiety-driven state of fight or flight.

   Some of the ways anxiety can impact your physical health include increased risk of high blood pressure and heart disease, lowered immunity, headaches, muscle tension, and insomnia.

   Your response: Have you experienced physical symptoms as a result of anxiety? If so, what kind of symptoms have you experienced?

   _____

   _____

   _____

   _____

Taking Stock

If nutritious food, water, sleep, nutrients, and gut health can improve your mood and lessen anxiety, are you paying attention to signs that your body may be lacking these things? Is your body telling you it needs more sleep or water or that your gut health is out of balance? Here are some signs to watch for.

Indicators that you may not be getting enough sleep:
- Yawning
- Moodiness
- Falling asleep during the day
- Irritability
- Brain fog
- Poor balance

Indicators that you are dehydrated:
- Thirst
- Fine lines and uneven tone of skin
- Brain fog
- Bad breath
- Dark urine
- Dizziness/low blood pressure

Indicators that you need to take better care of your gut health:
- Eczema
- Autoimmune issues
- Food intolerances
- A diet of sugary and processed foods
- Heartburn, gas, and bloating
- Sugar cravings
- Anxiety and depression

Change Your Story, Change Your Life

1. Describe the story you have told yourself about your relationship with your body. Is healthy eating and exercise something you consider punishment? Something you feel guilty about doing? Something to avoid? Write it all out—just let it flow without self-editing or filtering.

    _____

    _____

    _____

    _____

    _____

    _____

    _____

    _____

    _____

    _____

2. Now write out a different narrative you want to embrace. Where do you want to end up? Describe your ideal future and destination.

    _____

    _____

    _____

    _____

    _____

    _____

    _____

    _____

    _____

Dig Deeper

1. Describe what you currently do to take care of your body and your health.

    _____

    _____

    _____

    _____

    _____

2. Approximately how many hours a week do you devote to taking care of yourself? This can include exercising and preparing healthy meals. This can also include stress-reducing activities like walking in nature, getting a massage, going on a date night with your spouse, and spending time in prayer and meditation. How do you feel after engaging in these self-care activities?

    _____

    _____

    _____

    _____

    _____

3. Do you have consistent evening rituals that help you wind down your day and prepare for a good night's sleep? If you do, list them below. If you do not, list three things you could do that would help you wind down your day and get a better night's sleep.

    _____

    _____

    _____

    _____

    _____

4. Taking a pill to reduce anxiety may seem like a simple solution, but it's not the only solution (nor is it always the best solution). Making lifestyle changes can make a huge difference in your emotions, but they are more work than turning to medication. How willing are you to make lifestyle changes that may improve the quality of your life?

_____

_____

_____

_____

_____

5. Based on what you've read in this workbook and in *The Anxiety Reset*, what are three doable ways you can work to improve your health (and your mood) this week? What are three longer-term goals for improving your health?

_____

_____

_____

_____

_____

First Steps, Next Steps

Now it's time to get practical. We've explored many issues that prompted you to ponder and process. Let's put those thoughts into action. I'll provide several steps forward, and then it's your turn to determine three additional actions you will take this week.

1. Chapter 13 of *The Anxiety Reset* identifies five actions you can take to improve your health. If you haven't read the book, I encourage you to do so—and to take the actions in this chapter. Like this one:

Research what types of prebiotics, probiotics, and mood-improvement supplements might be best for you. By no means am I trying to push The Center's products on you, but they are an option for you to consider. Our team of experts has worked with a nutritional-supplement company to produce a range of products that we believe are very helpful. Another option is to visit your trusted health-food store, one that has a good nutrition section, preferably with a nutrition specialist on staff.

If you haven't taken this action, do it now.

From your research and consultations, what supplements do you think your body is lacking? What probiotic solutions are you adding to your diet? Natural foods containing probiotics include live culture yogurts, kefir, sauerkraut, and kimchi. Probiotic supplements are also effective. What actions are you taking—or are you willing to take—to improve the health of your "second brain"?

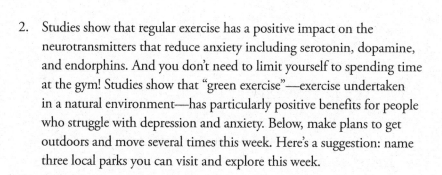

2. Studies show that regular exercise has a positive impact on the neurotransmitters that reduce anxiety including serotonin, dopamine, and endorphins. And you don't need to limit yourself to spending time at the gym! Studies show that "green exercise"—exercise undertaken in a natural environment—has particularly positive benefits for people who struggle with depression and anxiety. Below, make plans to get outdoors and move several times this week. Here's a suggestion: name three local parks you can visit and explore this week.

3. How much water should you really be drinking? A good rule of thumb is to divide your weight in two to determine how many ounces of water you should be drinking. Keep in mind that when you exercise or live in a hot climate, your hydration needs will be even greater. Below, calculate based on your weight the minimum amount of water your body needs and commit to drinking that many ounces every day this week.

4. Your turn. What steps do you intend to take this week to move toward wellness?

   a.

   b.

   c.

Closing Reflections

Your body is amazingly resilient. You might think that you've neglected your health for too long to make a real difference at this stage in your life, but that's far from true.

The truth is that getting more sleep and staying hydrated create nearly immediate improvements in energy, mood, and overall health.

Your gut health is resilient too. You won't see improvements as immediately as you will after a good night's sleep, but eating the right food and taking the right supplements over time can bring your microbiome back into balance. And regular exercise improves your health at every age and stage of life.

Will these efforts "cure" anxiety? No, but they will go a long way toward addressing underlying contributors and giving your energy and mood a significant boost at the same time.

Meditate on This Scripture

The LORD gives strength to his people;
    the LORD blesses his people with peace.

PSALM 29:11

Wise Words to Awaken Your Spirit

Exercise and application produce order in our affairs, health of body, cheerfulness of mind, and these make us precious to our friends.

THOMAS JEFFERSON

Journal Your Journey

This week you are going to be trying out new things, taking steps forward, forging new habits, and letting go of old ones. Will these things make a difference? Will you be able to discern any changes in how you feel and what you think?

This space is here for you to journal about the journey. What works? What doesn't? You'll know what to keep doing because you'll have your adventure documented in the pages of this workbook. Use this space to ask questions, make lists, doodle, write about your progress, and record milestones.

Let the adventure begin!

Find Strength in Soul Care

Nourish your spiritual life to find serenity.

■ **Review chapter 16 in *The Anxiety Reset* book.**

Week 9 at a Glance

Every person on earth is a dynamic integration of physical, emotional, mental, and spiritual components. We achieve health and well-being when each of these aspects is attended to and when all are in balance with the others.

This is why I believe strongly that nurturing your soul is just as essential as nurturing your body, mind, and emotions. I appreciate the words of scientist and philosopher Carl Sagan, who wrote, "Science is not only compatible with spirituality; it is a profound source of spirituality." And spirituality, in turn, is a profound source of healing and comfort to people struggling with the challenges posed by anxiety.

Soul care will not solve the challenges of anxiety overnight. Like every other strategy that I have presented, caring for your soul is a choice that takes dedication and determination. However, nurturing the spiritual dimension of your life will unlock the inner resources that make everything else easier. If you must choose only one thing to do for yourself right now, let it be this: "Seek first [God's] kingdom and his righteousness, and all these things [that you need] will be given to you as well" (Matthew 6:33).

Essential Ideas . . . and Your Insights

1. **Hope fuels everything.** Without hope, we stop asking questions, digging for answers, and pursuing anything, including our own wellness. After all, if we do not believe something is possible, why even try?

    You may feel devoid of hope. But I'm going to step out on a limb and say that you are more hopeful than you think you are. If hope is the fuel that empowers us to try anything at all, just the fact that you are on week 9 of this workbook speaks volumes. (Even if you skipped weeks 1 through 8, it doesn't matter: you are still here.)

    So you have hope. And even a little bit of hope goes a long, long way.

    Your response: We have all experienced times when we felt hopeless that change was possible. And yet, very often, even seemingly hopeless situations in our lives can turn out far more joyfully than we imagined. Can you identify a challenge that you overcame, despite feeling that things were hopeless? How did you do it?

    _____

    _____

    _____

    _____

    _____

2. **We can get messages from society (and those around us) that fly in the face of life-giving truths.** When we embrace life-giving truths, we are filled with hope. When society (and even loved ones) convince us to reject these truths, we feel hopeless.

    Here are four important truths that foster hope in the human spirit:

- I am not alone.
- I am loved.
- I have a purpose.
- I can approach God for help.

Your response: Of the four truths listed above, which do you believe? Which do you struggle to believe? Why?

_____

_____

_____

_____

_____

3. **The health of our souls is not a random thing that happens to us.** It is not beyond our control to improve or change. There are, in fact, actions we can take every day that will leave us stronger, more hopeful, and more connected to others and to our Creator. Taking good care of your soul is a lifelong journey, and the benefits are game-changing, now and even into eternity.

   Your response: When you think of soul care, what comes to mind? What actions do you think might fall into the category of soul care? How many of these actions do you take on a regular basis?

   _____

   _____

   _____

   _____

   _____

Taking Stock

Indicate below how regularly you engage in the following practices. Then write three additional actions that nurture your soul and indicate how often you practice them in your life:

- 1 = very little
- 2 = often but not regularly
- 3 = on a daily basis

1. Praying   1   2   3
2. Expressing gratitude to God or to others   1   2   3
3. Forgiving those who have hurt you in the past   1   2   3
4. Practicing generosity with others   1   2   3
5. _____   1   2   3
6. _____   1   2   3
7. _____   1   2   3

Change Your Story, Change Your Life

1. Describe what you have believed about your soul and your spiritual journey so far. If you have beliefs that you suspect are untrue (or hope are untrue), how did you come by these beliefs in the first place? Write out your story—just let it flow without self-editing or filtering.

2. Now write out a different narrative you want to embrace. Where do you want to end up? Describe your ideal future and destination.

_____

_____

_____

_____

_____

_____

Dig Deeper

1. What do you think about the idea that you are not alone, that there is a loving God who longs for a relationship (or perhaps a deeper relationship) with you? How might this change how you live your life or how you feel about your life?

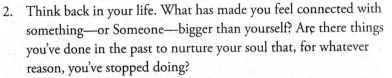

2. Think back in your life. What has made you feel connected with something—or Someone—bigger than yourself? Are there things you've done in the past to nurture your soul that, for whatever reason, you've stopped doing?

    These might include walks in nature, going to church, praying, reading books, keeping a gratitude journal, playing an instrument, worshipping, or volunteering or ministering in your community. Perhaps there was a season in your life when your soul felt nurtured because you were in a community that focused on these things.

    Let your mind wander back through the years, and see if there are things that at one time helped your spirit thrive which are no longer a part of your life. Record those things here.

3. Review your list above. How did these healthy, soulful activities fade from your life? What changed? What would happen if you began doing one or more of these things again?

4. What role does unforgiveness play in your life? Are there past hurts you can't seem to release? How do you think unforgiveness is impacting your current joy, relationships, hope, and perspective?

5. If a friend of yours was holding a grudge toward someone who had hurt them in the past and you could see that your friend was missing out on peace and joy by holding on to their bitterness, what advice would you have for them?

First Steps, Next Steps

Now it's time to get practical. We've explored many issues that prompted you to ponder and process. Let's put those thoughts into action. I'll provide several steps forward, and then it's your turn to determine three additional actions you will take this week.

1. Chapter 16 of *The Anxiety Reset* identifies five actions you can take to nurture your soul. If you haven't read the book, I encourage you to do so—and to take the actions in this chapter. Like this one:

    > Ask for God's guidance. One of the most mistaken ideas about spiritual renewal is that you must find your way through the door on your own. As I pointed out earlier, you are not alone. That means help is available, even if what you need is help finding help. Ask. You'll be amazed at the result.

    If you haven't taken this action, do it now.

    Once you have asked God for guidance, consider the following questions. What do you think guidance from God looks like—or will look like if you have yet to sense it? Are you listening for his voice in new ways? Have you surrounded yourself with others who believe in him and seek direction and help from him?

2. Studies show that when we actively engage in feelings of gratitude, it improves our relationships, sleep, mood, self-esteem, happiness, and even our health. We become less materialistic, less impatient, and we even make better decisions.

    Some people practice gratitude on a daily basis through journaling, affirmations, counting a long list of blessings, or simply naming three things they are thankful for every time they begin to feel anxious or irritable.

What is one way you could experience and practice gratitude more often? What would that look like in your life?

_____

_____

_____

_____

3. Plan a day of solitude. When we are glued to our phones, computers, social media, or texts from friends, the noise never stops. With all the distractions, we can find it increasingly difficult to connect with our own souls, much less with God. Plan a day of solitude. Unplug. Read. Pray. Think. Listen. In the space below, identify a day you can do this, and describe what actions you are going to take to give yourself the gift of space and time to tend to your soul.

_____

_____

_____

_____

4. Your turn. What steps do you intend to take this week to move toward wellness?

   a. _____

_____

_____

   b. _____

_____

_____

c. ....

....

....

Closing Reflections

Some people are afraid to spend time alone with their thoughts or with God. Reflecting on the statements we examined at the beginning of this week—I am not alone, I am loved, I have a purpose, I can approach God for help—can feel threatening.

Taking time to nurture your soul may feel pointless if you have already abandoned hope. But don't give up.

We were created to experience spiritual life and soul health. If this idea seems uncomfortable to you, ask God to help you in the journey to discover all that you were created to enjoy and become.

Meditate on This Scripture

Those who hope in the LORD
will renew their strength.

ISAIAH 40:31

Wise Words to Awaken Your Spirit

Hope is the thing with feathers that perches in the soul, and sings the tune without the words, and never stops at all.

EMILY DICKINSON

Journal Your Journey

This week you are going to be trying out new things, taking steps forward, forging new habits, and letting go of old ones. Will these things make a difference? Will you be able to discern any changes in how you feel and what you think?

This space is here for you to journal about the journey. What works? What doesn't? You'll know what to keep doing because you'll have your adventure documented in the pages of this workbook. Use this space to ask questions, make lists, doodle, write about your progress, and record milestones.

Let the adventure begin!

Become Bold & Brave

Can you really be free from worry? The answer is yes!

▨ **Review chapter 17 in** *The Anxiety Reset* **book.**

Week 10 at a Glance

Among the many things Jesus is reported to have told people in his day, one message is repeated again and again: *Don't be afraid. Don't worry. Put down your burden and rest.*

No matter who you are, that sounds like a very positive and healthy way to live. We all fear something and from time to time get caught in the whirlpool of worrying about life's "what-ifs." But to people who struggle with extreme anxiety, life without fear can sound far *too* good—and very hard to believe. When every day is one long battle with crippling dread, simply hearing the words "Fear not" can hit you like fingernails on a chalkboard. "Yeah, right," you respond. "That's easy to *say*! But it can't be done."

The bad news in that is you are unlikely to work toward something you believe to be impossible, and what we don't attempt, we can't achieve. But here's the good news: you haven't come this far in your search for healing only to slam the door now. Reading this book is proof that you are ready to enter new territory and think things you've never thought before. You're willing to consider that you've been wrong about what is possible and what isn't—that the way you've been living until now is not the only way you *can* live. You're tired of being bullied and backed into a corner by fear, and you are ready to fight back.

Essential Ideas . . . and Your Insights

1. **When you are paralyzed by anxiety, what you actually fear is the feeling of being afraid.** It isn't heights, enclosed spaces, social awkwardness, or any of the myriad triggers people believe to be the source of their fear. What we are desperate to avoid in all those cases is how lousy fear feels.

   Your response: How would it change your attitude about your fears to realize what you are conditioned to avoid is the feeling of fear itself, not the thing or activity that triggers it? Make a list of reasons why that's a *very* big distinction.

   _____

   _____

   _____

   _____

   _____

2. **Centering your awareness in the present moment—and letting your focus on what is real right now distract your mind from the past and future fantasies—is a great way to silence your fears and find rest.** If you habitually spend time imagining frightening or traumatic events in the past or future, your body responds exactly as if that event is really happening. But because it's not real, there is no natural closure to your heightened state of alarm, exposing your body to harmful stress hormones over long periods of time. The consequences of that include a whole host of physical ailments, not to mention the tragedy of your lost enjoyment of life.

   Your response: Imagine an event in your past or one you fear might occur in the future that causes you anxiety. Is there any reason to believe it poses any *present danger*—right here, right now? Is it helpful or healthy for your body to be tense and stressed over something that is not happening now? Describe what it feels like when you imagine the event.

_____

_____

_____

_____

_____

3. **Walking toward what makes you afraid—in a safe and controlled way—is a proven way to drain your fear of its potency.** It is called "exposure therapy"—the psychological equivalent of inoculation. We all understand that vaccines contain small amounts of the very diseases we hope to eradicate. The idea is to train your immune system how to handle tiny doses so that when a full onslaught happens, it's prepared for the worst. In the same way, your mind can be taught courage and resilience through controlled exposure to frightening circumstances.

    Your response: What does the idea of being "exposed" to the things you fear make you feel? What price would you pay to gain the upper hand on your fear and anxiety?

_____

_____

_____

_____

_____

Taking Stock

Use the following prompts to examine your fears more closely and to find ways to calm them.

I am most afraid of:

    1.

    2.

    3.

    4.

When I am in the grip of my fear, I feel:
    (Include physical sensations and emotions.)

    1.

    2.

    3.

    4.

Once my fear is triggered, I no longer feel able to:

    1.

    2.

    3.

    4.

When I'm experiencing fear, what I really want to say to people is:

    1.

    2.

    3.

    4.

Four strategies I know will help diffuse my fear, if I choose to employ
    them:

    1.

    2.

    3.

    4.

When I think about what fearfulness has cost me, I feel:

1.

2.

3.

4.

What I will lose if I let go of my fear:

1.

2.

3.

4.

What I will gain if I let go of my fear:

1.

2.

3.

4.

Four courageous *actions* I could take to assert power over my fear:

1.

2.

3.

4.

If I were not so afraid, I would:

1.

2.

3.

4.

Change Your Story, Change Your Life

1. What is the story you tell yourself about your fear? What is its origin? When did you begin to alter your life in response to your fear? Describe some experiences when your fear caused you to miss out on something important. Write out your story—just let it flow without self-editing or filtering.

2. Now write out a different narrative you want to embrace. Where do you want to end up? Describe your ideal life, free of fear.

Dig Deeper

1. What is your earliest memory surrounding your fearfulness? How
    did it begin? Does telling the story now—given what you are
    learning about anxiety and wellness—make you feel differently
    about it? How?

2. How has fear been a force in your life? Describe a time when fear
    served as a positive emotion for you (perhaps helping you avoid
    danger or prepare for a challenge). Next describe a time when
    it was counterproductive (perhaps causing you to limit your
    experience of life in order to play it safe).

3. If you were to courageously face your fears today, what's the
    worst thing that might happen? What's the best thing that might
    happen?

4. What would you like others to understand about your experience of living with fear? How would you advise them to help you? Put yourself in their position. What do you imagine others would like *you* to know about *their* experience watching you limit your life in the face of your fear?

_____

_____

_____

_____

_____

_____

5. As you consider the negative effects of your fear, what goals would you set for yourself—large or small—to begin taking back your life?

_____

_____

_____

_____

_____

_____

First Steps, Next Steps

Now it's time to get practical. We've explored many issues that prompted you to ponder and process. Let's put those thoughts into action. I'll provide several steps forward, and then it's your turn to determine three other steps you will take this week.

1. Name your fears. Chances are, you've gotten very good at avoiding the things that make you afraid. Even thinking of them can trigger a fear response, so you've learned to not do that either. This strategy

only serves to deepen your anxiety and prolong your recovery. Reverse it by writing down all the things that have paralyzed you, honestly and clearly:

2. Revisit a time when fear created a hardship in your life. Write about the experience, and create a new ending to the story.

3. Write a note to yourself describing how you would ideally like to handle your fear in the future.

4. Your turn. What steps do you intend to take this week to move toward wellness?

    a.

b.

c.

Closing Reflections

Elevators are not your enemy, nor are spiders or public speaking or financial calamity. As President Roosevelt rightly said in an address to the nation during the Great Depression, it is fear itself. Sometime in your past you associated those things with pain and trauma. You learned to expect an unpleasant fearful response when your particular trigger appeared. The good news—the *very* good news—is that it's possible to *un*learn that now.

To do that, you will need to stop running away and face your fear head-on. As another Roosevelt—Eleanor—once said, "You gain strength, courage, and confidence by every experience in which you really stop to look fear in the face. You are able to say to yourself, 'I lived through this horror. I can take the next thing that comes along.'"

Meditate on This Scripture

Do not fear, for I am with you;
  do not be dismayed, for I am your God.
I will strengthen you and help you;
    I will uphold you with my righteous right hand.
ISAIAH 41:10

Wise Words to Awaken Your Spirit

Of all the liars in the world, sometimes the worst are our own fears.
RUDYARD KIPLING

Journal Your Journey

This week you are going to be trying out new things, taking steps forward, forging new habits, and letting go of old ones. Will these things make a difference? Will you be able to discern any changes in how you feel and what you think?

This space is here for you to journal about the journey. What works? What doesn't? You'll know what to keep doing because you'll have your adventure documented in the pages of this workbook. Use this space to ask questions, make lists, doodle, write about your progress, and record milestones.

Let the adventure begin!

Sanity through Simplicity

Decrease and release to find peace.

▪ **Review chapter 18 in *The Anxiety Reset* book.**

Week 11 at a Glance

Our brains love order. Clutter, however, disrupts the mental processes we use to focus, process, and create. Clutter also fosters feelings of guilt, distraction, overwhelm, shame, and frustration.

In addition, when we are surrounded by things that are too much to manage, it can trigger the release of the stress hormone cortisol.

Cortisol is beneficial to our bodies—in the right doses. For example, it provides a burst of energy in times of danger, lowers our sensitivity to pain, and boosts our immune system. For these reasons, our cortisol levels are typically higher in the morning, when we need to tackle our day, and lower in the evenings, when it's time to relax.

But when we live under constant stress—like the stress created by ongoing clutter—our bodies don't get a chance to rest from the stimulating effects of cortisol. Increased cortisol levels—especially over a long period of time—have myriad side effects, including higher blood pressure, increased heart rate, impaired immunity, increased belly fat, and even impaired cognitive function. For example, women with elevated cortisol levels show smaller brain volume, while men and women with higher cortisol levels show impaired memory function.

Can simplifying your life reduce your stress and improve your health—and your emotions—in the process?

You bet it can.

Essential Ideas . . . and Your Insights

1. **Simplicity is a state of mind.** It's tempting to think that selling everything and living in an off-grid cabin—far away from our current stressors, drama, and distractions—would give us the simple, unfettered lives we crave.

    We can also fall into the temptation of thinking that if we were only to go back in time, living in a technologically simpler era would allow us to live slower, less cluttered lives.

    But simplicity is as much a mindset as a lifestyle, and it requires a level of inner work to achieve what we desire. Escaping isn't the answer.

    But you *can* simplify your life, no cabins or time machines required.

    Your response: When you think about decluttering your life, what fantasy scenarios do you envision? Moving to another state? A different century? Are you convinced that winning the lottery would simplify your life? Do you envision a simpler life in the future, perhaps when the kids are grown and your nest is empty? Write your thoughts below.

    _____

    _____

    _____

    _____

2. **Simplicity isn't about getting rid of material "stuff."** That being said, getting rid of things can play an important role in the process of simplifying our lives.

No, simplifying our lives entails ridding ourselves of any kind of chaos and clutter holding us back. Our relationships, finances, emotions, self-talk, diets, and calendars can all become sources of unnecessary chaos and drama. The good news is that we can simplify our lives in these areas too.

Your response: When you think of clutter in your life, do your thoughts go immediately to your closets, garage, and junk drawers? What are some other areas in your life where you feel like you have no margin or space in which to move or breathe?

_____

_____

_____

_____

3. **When it comes to simplifying your life, less is more. But having less is only the beginning.** Other ways to embrace "less" include _knowing_ less (e.g., turning off the news), _connecting_ less online, _eating_ less, and _doing_ less.

    Your response: Can you think of other things you could do with less of in your life? Include some suggestions here.

_____

_____

_____

_____

Taking Stock

Take the clutter quiz! How many of these statements apply to you? And as you look over this list, can you see how physical clutter contributes to stress and anxiety in your life?

- You feel cramped by clutter.
- The furniture in your house is covered by stuff.

- When you buy new things, it's hard to find a place to put them when you bring them home from the store.
- You save used food containers in case you need them later.
- Getting dressed in the morning is stressful because your clothes are in piles and are often too wrinkled to wear.
- You can't find things you need (financial papers, car keys, tools) when you need them and are consistently late to things (or miss important deadlines) as a result.
- You have multiples of the same items because when you can't find what you need when you need it, you buy it again.
- There are areas of your house you would be embarrassed for people to see.
- Having people over for the holidays or entertaining out-of-town guests is exhausting because it requires a day-long cleaning blitz.
- When you clean, you focus more on finding new places to stash things than getting rid of things.
- You struggle with feelings of inferiority because you're convinced other people have better organized lives than you.
- You fantasize about systems that will help you tame the clutter in your life but struggle to implement them.
- When you do create a system to help you simplify your life, you don't maintain it past a few weeks or days.
- You can't put things away in closets and drawers because these storage zones are already overflowing with heaven knows what.

Change Your Story, Change Your Life

1. Describe your relationship with clutter of all kinds. What has your story been? Just let it flow without self-editing or filtering.

   _____

   _____

   _____

_____

_____

_____

_____

_____

2. Now write out a different narrative you want to embrace. Where do you want to end up? Describe your ideal future and destination.

_____

_____

_____

_____

_____

_____

_____

_____

Dig Deeper

1. What is clutter? Clutter can consist of things you've never needed, things that were helpful once but are now unnecessary or even detrimental to you, or things you never wanted but were given to you by other people. Perhaps clutter is too much of a good thing. Clutter might even be something that's extremely valuable—but not to you. Maybe clutter is anything holding you back from the life you want to live. How do *you* define "clutter"?

_____

_____

_____

_____

_____

2. Can you see how the above definitions of clutter can apply to more than just physical stuff? When you apply those same definitions to nontangible things like thoughts, beliefs, emotions, time, to-do lists, and relationships, do they resonate with you? Why or why not?

_____

_____

_____

_____

3. Are there painful or limiting beliefs you hold about yourself that were handed down to you by others? If you thought of these beliefs as clutter, would it be easier to get rid of them? Explain.

_____

_____

_____

_____

4. Do you find yourself saying, "Things are only hectic right now; life will be simpler when . . ."? How long have you been telling yourself that? Is it possible that life will never feel simpler on its own without some intentional decluttering and restructuring on your part? Use this space to respond to that possibility.

_____

_____

_____

_____

5. What is cluttering your calendar or to-do list? Do you agree to too many obligations? Do you give yourself permission to say no to things you know you don't have time for? Describe your idea of an enjoyable, simplified day. How different is that from how you typically spend your days?

_____

_____

_____

_____

_____

First Steps, Next Steps

Now it's time to get practical. We've explored many issues that prompted you to ponder and process. Let's put those thoughts into action. I'll provide several steps forward, and then it's your turn to determine three additional actions you will take this week.

1. Chapter 18 of *The Anxiety Reset* identifies five actions you can take to simplify your life. If you haven't read the book, I encourage you to do so—and to take the actions in this chapter. Like this one:

    Do less. Look at your calendar. Clutter comes in many forms—including excessive busyness. Are any of your obligations there simply to distract you and fill time or to fulfill someone else's idea of what you "should" be doing? If so, consider making a new commitment to yourself and eliminate at least one optional activity a day.

    If you haven't taken this action, do it now.
    What optional activity did you identify? As you free up space in your day, resist the temptation to fill that space with another activity or item on your to-do list. Once you've done this for several days, what does it feel like? What thoughts do you have

about the experience? Can you think of additional ways to declutter your schedule?

_____

_____

_____

_____

_____

2. Forgive someone. Hurt and anger are not necessarily wrong or right; they just are. They are often stages in a process that begins with being wronged and ultimately—hopefully—leads to healing. But when our hurt and anger stop being "stages" and turn into something we embrace for years (or for a lifetime!), they have outlived their usefulness and turned into an unnecessary burden. They've entered the realm of emotional clutter.

    Forgiving someone doesn't mean what they did is okay. It does mean freeing yourself from being the keeper of the memory of the pain. Whom do you need to forgive? What steps do you need to take to let go of the hurt and anger?

_____

_____

_____

_____

_____

3. Make time every day to take stock and toss what you no longer need. This doesn't have to be overwhelming. In fact, it might be as simple as a five-minute check-in with your emotions, schedule, and surroundings and then taking one simple action.

    Can you simplify your life by looking around the room and finding one thing to throw away or take to a donation center? Is there a negative thought that's been cluttering your head that you can banish? Would it simplify your life to stop procrastination and walk over to your desk and pay that nagging bill?

Over time, taking a single decluttering action every day will add up. Name something you can get rid of today:

_____

_____

_____

_____

4. Your turn. What steps do you intend to take this week to move toward wellness?

a. _____

_____

_____

b. _____

_____

_____

c. _____

_____

_____

Closing Reflections

Our lives will never be stress free, nor should they be. In fact, stress can actually motivate us and help us meet the challenges of life.

Plus, stress is unavoidable. So are distractions. And seasons of having to cope with "too much" stuff, emotions, commitments, drama in relationships—are part and parcel of a full and fulfilling life.

That said, why sign up for more of it than we need to experience? There's much in life we can't control. Clutter doesn't need to be one of those things.

If you are dealing with clutter in your home, thoughts, emotions, time, body, or relationships, practice the habit of letting go. And if you find you can't manage it on your own, don't hesitate to seek help. Take a course. Hire a professional organizer. Find a counselor. Read a book. Invite a wise friend into your journey. Pray and ask God for help too.

Life is too short and too precious to spend it managing stuff we can do without.

Meditate on This Scripture

Do not worry about your life, what you will eat or drink; or about your body, what you will wear. Is not life more than food, and the body more than clothes? Look at the birds of the air; they do not sow or reap or store away in barns, and yet your heavenly Father feeds them. Are you not much more valuable than they?

MATTHEW 6:25-26

Wise Words to Awaken Your Spirit

Voluntary simplicity means going fewer places in one day rather than more, seeing less so I can see more, doing less so I can do more, acquiring less so I can have more.

JON KABAT-ZINN

Journal Your Journey

This week you are going to be trying out new things, taking steps forward, forging new habits, and letting go of old ones. Will these things make a difference? Will you be able to discern any changes in how you feel and what you think?

This space is here for you to journal about the journey. What works? What doesn't? You'll know what to keep doing because you'll have your adventure documented in the pages of this workbook. Use this space to ask questions, make lists, doodle, write about your progress, and record milestones.

Let the adventure begin!

Back to a Better Future

Believe it! Your best life is still to come.

▪ **Review the epilogue in *The Anxiety Reset* book.**

Week 12 at a Glance

Now that we've reached the end of this journey together, it's time for me to reveal the secret agenda I have followed from page one. Every story, every research fact, every tip and suggestion has had a single purpose: I'm organizing a *jailbreak*.

I've never done time in prison, but I know firsthand that uncontrolled anxiety feels very much as if it's made of concrete walls and iron bars. I've lived with barbed wire coiled around my mind. I know how it feels when my own thoughts snarl and snap like vicious guard dogs. The punishment that prison is meant to be for actual inmates is the loss of freedom to live as they please and the reduction of their world to the size of a tiny cell. Anyone who has been backed by fear into a smaller and smaller life will instantly recognize the comparison.

In fact, it's not uncommon for prisoners serving a lengthy sentence to cut all ties with their former lives—with the people, memories, and, most of all, everything they've ever dreamed of having, doing, or being. It's too painful to consider those things, so they do their best to simply stop.

People suffering the crippling effects of anxiety often make a similar choice. They feel they've been given a life sentence and have no right to hope for better.

If that describes you or someone you love, then I've got startling news: it's high time to bust out of there. In previous chapters, you have gathered the tools you need to be free once more. It's time for you to decide: Are you with me?

Essential Ideas . . . and Your Insights

1. **Believe a better life is possible.** For many people, especially those conditioned by fear and anxiety to avoid uncomfortable risk, just about everything seems impossible. Some days, that includes getting out of bed in the morning. So the idea that the day ahead might include full-fledged escape from the prison of anxiety seems about as likely as sprouting wings and flying.

    But *faith* is nothing if not the belief that, with God, anything is possible!

    Your response: Visualize your life without the burden of anxiety—full, free, and healthy. Which parts of that picture seem impossible to you today? Are you willing to consider you may be wrong about that?

    _____

    _____

    _____

    _____

2. **Think of nothing else.** Once you've chosen to truly believe that you can be free from anxiety—and that a happy, healthy life is possible outside the walls of fear—then visualize it with all you've got. Tenaciously. Ferociously. Faith is not a feeling that comes and goes on its own like the tide; it's an active choice. It is a *discipline*. If you

were on the inside of an actual prison and had decided to mount an escape, it would be all too easy to notice only the apparent reasons for inevitable failure: walls, towers, guards, dogs, bars, locks. In other words, it would be easy to focus on *what is* rather than on *what can be.* To avoid that trap, employ one of the most powerful tools in your kit: your imagination.

Your response: Take a look at your habitual thought life. Where do you spend the most time—imagining and planning for new possibilities, or mulling over everything your mind says can't be done? Explain.

---

3. **Never give up.** Early Spanish explorers sometimes burned the ships that had carried their party across the Atlantic. Though I'd never recommend anything that dramatic in your life, there is something to be learned from the mindset that commits completely to what lies ahead. When some part of your plan doesn't work as you had thought, don't let that send you back into your cell of old patterns of defeat. Immediately begin drawing up a new strategy. Lower your shoulder and get back in there.

I'll say it again: the stakes are high. Your determination must be higher.

Your response: In your struggle with anxiety, have you allowed failure to get the upper hand and discourage you? Can you recall times when you refused to give up on a goal you had set? How did it make you feel to succeed in spite of wanting to quit?

Taking Stock

Use the following prompts to help you plan your jailbreak.

I am tired of living in bondage to anxiety because:

1.

2.

3.

4.

When I think of life on the other side of healing,
I look forward to:

1.

2.

3.

4.

Here are the names of some accomplices I know I'll need for my
jailbreak:

1.

2.

3.

4.

Four essential parts of my jailbreak plan:

1.

2.

3.

4.

When setbacks come, I promise myself I will:

1.

2.

3.

4.

Four jailbreak skills I know I possess:

1.

2.

3.

4.

The walls of my anxiety prison cell aren't made of brick but of
thoughts, such as:

1.

2.

3.

4.

Four things I've accomplished (no matter how small) that at first
seemed impossible:

1.

2.

3.

4.

Four ways I plan to ignore the prison and focus on life outside the walls:

1.

2.

3.

4.

Reasons to believe that with God, all things are possible:

1.

2.

3.

4.

Change Your Story, Change Your Life

1. What story do you tell yourself about the power of anxiety to lock you away from a more free and healthy life? In that narrative, what are the walls made of? Who stands guard at the gates? Write out your story—just let it flow without self-editing or filtering.

   _____

   _____

   _____

   _____

   _____

   _____

   _____

2. Now write out a different story you want to embrace. Where do you want to end up? Describe your ideal life, free of anxiety.

   _____

   _____

   _____

   _____

   _____

   _____

   _____

Dig Deeper

1. In what ways has anxiety caused your life to shrink to the size of a prison cell? Can you recall a time before anxiety took hold? Describe it. What does thinking about that time make you feel?

2. What do you think of the "jailbreak" analogy? Are you ready to believe that such decisive change is possible? Why or why not?

3. What possible payoffs do you experience by remaining stuck in anxiety? Does it frighten you to think of giving them up? Explain.

4. Do you worry that you have lost the ability to live without fear? Is that a good reason to stay where you are? Describe the risks you think freedom entails.

5. What personal goals and dreams form your greatest source of determination to succeed at the jailbreak? What strategies do you have for keeping those things in focus through hard times?

_____

_____

_____

_____

_____

First Steps, Next Steps

Now it's time to get practical. We've explored many issues that prompted you to ponder and process. Let's put those thoughts into action. I'll provide several steps forward, and then it's your turn to determine three other steps you will take this week.

1. Draw up a fictitious floor plan of the prison that anxiety has formed around your life. Label the walls, gates, guard towers, and barbed wire fences with names that identify your real-life fears and stressors. Now make notes and sketches describing how you plan to get past them in your escape. Have as much fun as possible. Watch caper and escape movies for inspiration.

2. Write letters to important people in your life letting them know of your intention to bust out of prison. Let them know exactly how they can help. List here the people you'll write to.

_____

_____

_____

_____

_____

3. Make a list of things you plan to do once you're free—things you've dreamed of during your years of captivity. Be as specific as possible.

_____

_____

_____

_____

_____

4. Your turn. What steps do you intend to take this week to move toward wellness?

a. _____

_____

_____

b. _____

_____

_____

c. _____

_____

_____

Closing Reflections

It's not possible to overstate the prize that awaits as a reward for all this effort. You never deserved to be locked away behind the walls of anxiety and fear. Like everyone else on earth, you were born to be happy, healthy, and free.

Throughout *The Anxiety Reset* book and workbook, you've explored the many interwoven causes and effects of uncontrolled anxiety. Some of those contributing factors you unwittingly chose for yourself—like diet, substance use, unbalanced use of technology, and so on. Others came to you as a biological inheritance, an unwanted challenge to overcome. In every case, however, you now know there are tools available to help you break your chains and finally possess what you've been looking for: freedom from fear.

Your positive future awaits!

Meditate on This Scripture

It is for freedom that Christ has set us free. Stand firm, then, and do not let yourselves be burdened again by a yoke of slavery.

GALATIANS 5:1

Wise Words to Awaken Your Spirit

If we all did the things we are really capable of doing, we would literally astound ourselves.

THOMAS A. EDISON

Journal Your Journey

This week you are going to be trying out new things, taking steps forward, forging new habits, and letting go of old ones. Will these things make a difference? Will you be able to discern any changes in how you feel and what you think?

This space is here for you to journal about the journey. What works? What doesn't? You'll know what to keep doing because you'll have your adventure documented in the pages of this workbook. Use this space to ask questions, make lists, doodle, write about your progress, and record milestones.

Let the adventure begin!

Notes

1. Tim Newman, "Anxiety in the West: Is It on the Rise?" *Medical News Today*, September 5, 2018, https://www.medicalnewstoday.com/articles/322877#Why-does-U.S.-society-breed-anxiety?.
2. "About ADAA: Facts and Statistics," Anxiety and Depression Association of America, https://adaa.org/about-adaa/press-room/facts-statistics.
3. "About ADAA: Facts and Statistics."

About the Authors

Mental health expert **Dr. Gregory Jantz** pioneered whole-person, holistic care. Now recognized as one of the leaders in holistic treatment, Dr. Jantz continues to identify more effective, cutting-edge forms of treatment for people struggling with eating disorders, depression, anxiety, and trauma. He is the founder of The Center: A Place of Hope, which was voted one of the top 10 facilities in the United States for the treatment of depression.

Dr. Jantz is a bestselling author of more than 37 books. He is a go-to media source for a range of behavioral-based afflictions, including drug and alcohol addictions. Dr. Jantz has appeared on CNN, FOX, ABC, and CBS and has been interviewed for the *New York Post*, Associated Press, *Forbes*, *Family Circle*, and *Woman's Day*. He is also a regular contributor to the *Thrive Global* and *Psychology Today* blogs. Visit www.aplaceofhope.com and www.drgregoryjantz.com.

Keith Wall, a twenty-five-year publishing veteran, is an award-winning author, magazine editor, radio scriptwriter, and online columnist. He currently writes full time in collaboration with several bestselling authors. Keith lives in a mountaintop cabin near Manitou Springs, Colorado.

Discover the tools to help you *overcome anxiety* so you can create a new, more *peace-filled life.*

Let Dr. Jantz, one of the foremost leaders in holistic health, guide you through the steps of discovering the mental, emotional, physical, and spiritual roots of anxiety to help you reclaim peace and joy for your future.